95

Strategies for
REMODELING
INSTRUCTION

LAURA E. PINTO • STEPHANIE SPARES • LAURA DRISCOLL

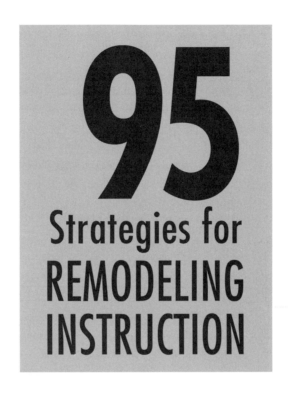

95
Strategies for
REMODELING
INSTRUCTION

IDEAS FOR INCORPORATING CCSS

CORWIN
A SAGE Company

CORWIN
A SAGE Company

FOR INFORMATION:

Corwin
A SAGE Company
2455 Teller Road
Thousand Oaks, California 91320
(800) 233-9936
Fax: (800) 417-2466
www.corwin.com

SAGE Ltd.
1 Oliver's Yard
55 City Road
London EC1Y 1SP
United Kingdom

SAGE Pvt. Ltd.
B 1/I 1 Mohan Cooperative Industrial Area
Mathura Road, New Delhi 110 044
India

SAGE Asia-Pacific Pte. Ltd.
33 Pekin Street #02-01
Far East Square
Singapore 048763

Acquisitions Editor: Hudson Perigo
Associate Editor: Allison Scott
Editorial Assistant: Lisa Whitney
Project Editor: Veronica Stapleton
Copy Editor: Lana Arndt
Typesetter: C&M Digitals (P) Ltd.
Proofreader: Scott Oney
Indexer: Molly Hall
Cover Designer: Michael Dubowe
Permissions Editor: Adele Hutchinson

Copyright © 2012 by Corwin

Printed in the United States of America

Library of Congress Cataloging-in-Publication Data

Pinto, Laura E.
95 strategies for remodeling instruction : ideas for incorporating CCSS / Laura E. Pinto, Stephanie Spares, Laura Driscoll.

p. cm.
Includes bibliographical references and index.

ISBN 978-1-4522-1875-5 (pbk.)

1. Education—Curricula—Standards—United States—States. 2. Effective teaching—United States. I. Spares, Stephanie. II. Driscoll, Laura. III. Title. IV. Title: Ninety-five strategies for remodeling instruction.

LB1570.P5525 2012
375′.001—dc23   2011040147

SUSTAINABLE FORESTRY INITIATIVE
Certified Chain of Custody
Promoting Sustainable Forestry
www.sfiprogram.org
SFI-01268

SFI label applies to text stock

12 13 14 15 16 10 9 8 7 6 5 4 3 2 1

Contents

Additional materials and resources related to *95 Strategies for Remodeling Instruction: Ideas for Incorporating CCSS* can be found at http://www.corwin.com/95strategies

Preface

Have you ever had a room or area in your home that was quite functional, perhaps attractive, but you had some ideas to make it even better? If so, you probably took on a remodeling project. Remodeling usually means we keep the useful and positive aspects of a space, but we improve on other aspects.

This book applies that very concept—remodeling—to instruction of students. As a teacher, you've probably developed many great lessons and units. And you probably have some that could be improved on too. This book provides you with a process to reflect on and critically analyze your instruction and the tools you need to refresh those lessons.

You'll begin the journey by first examining some of the evidence—research and best and promising practices—of what we know works when it comes to students' learning. This will provide you with the basis against which to analyze your lessons. Next, you'll learn about the process of remodeling and ways in which you can remodel either by yourself or with a group of peers in a professional learning community. Finally, just as you can't remodel a space without the right tools, you need tools for lesson remodeling as well. To achieve that, we offer you a compendium of 95 strategies to remodel your lessons, along with reproducibles where possible, to ensure that you can implement them in your classroom. These strategies are the tools you can use to efficiently and effectively remodel lessons for any subject and just about any grade level.

Using This Book

This book is designed to both outline processes and act as a reference guide. It has been piloted in various versions with more than 100 members of the education community and can be used in several ways:

Practitioner Uses

- For teachers planning a lesson or unit, who can flip through the compendium of strategies and select those they wish to use, inserting them directly into their lessons and making copies of the relevant reproducible
- When revising courses and lessons to remodel their existing lessons by flipping through the compendium of strategies and revising the lesson accordingly

College Faculty Uses

- A teaching tool and textbook to support preservice teachers' unit and lesson planning
- As a resource for inservice courses and workshops

District Uses

- A basis for professional development for teachers to guide lesson remodeling in workshop-driven inservice education
- As a basis to build professional learning communities aimed at improving instruction at either the school or district level

An Evidence-Based Approach

Research suggests that students retain only 20% of what they learn (Gardiner, 1998). Increasingly, we see calls for evidence-based practice (EBP) to define *what works* in education and inform practices in classrooms, schools, and districts. EBP is concerned with looking to research evidence to see what types of teaching/learning approaches are effective.

But what counts as evidence? The answer, which happens to be "many things," is a bit complicated. Evidence can be as simple as one teacher's experiences, where trial-and-error in the classroom can identify what works in *that* classroom, with *that* teacher, and with *those* students. Evidence can be as sophisticated as large-scale, international comparisons of teaching/learning approaches and their systemwide outcomes. The bottom line is that experience and analysis, together, lead to evidence, which can inform practice. However, as these examples suggest, some pieces of evidence are stronger than others. Figure 0.1 provides a guide to understanding the strength of evidence (adapted from Hyde, Falls, Morris, and Schoenwald's [2003] hierarchy for medical evidence). It should be noted that educational research is increasingly qualitative. When the research design is sound, both qualitative and quantitative studies can provide strong evidence, through very different types of useful information. In this book, we've drawn on evidence at just about all levels of the hierarchy.

Part of the teacher's role is to gather, assess, and apply evidence—in part, based on its strength, and in part, based on the teacher's professional judgment within his or her own classroom, school, and community. One caution to bear in mind is that though some evidence may be very sophisticated, this does not mean that it is applicable to other contexts. What works in the United Kingdom, for example, may not be appropriate for the United States. What works in rural Michigan might not work in urban Michigan. It's up to educators to analyze and make sense of the factors that may or may not make sense.

The authors have been mindful of using and applying evidence in the design of this book. In particular, the following important

Figure 0.1   Hierarchy of Evidence-Based Information

Higher level of evidence ↑	Experimental designs with control groups having random assignments that have been replicated in a variety of contexts	• In education, these typically appear in the academic literature; because education is a social science, not all phenomena can be controlled in this way.
	Experimental designs with control groups having random assignments that have only been investigated in one context	
	Evaluation of student outcomes; empirical (qualitative and quantitative) data collected from educational stakeholders	• Consumer feedback • Pilot tests of strategies and approaches
	Expert consensus agreement among a number of professionals; best practices	• Best practices achieved largely through professional discussion among teachers and PLCs but also through some published research
↓	Anecdotal evidence based on experiences of teachers or researchers; promising practice	• Action research publications • Professional discussion among teachers and PLCs
Lower level of evidence	Single-case studies, teachers' action research; promising practice	• Checklists and process charts established by individuals • Action research publications

NOTE: PLCs = professional learning communities.

evidence informs both the process of remodeling and the strategies we've included:

- Geoff Petty's (2009) extensive research into effective teaching suggests that a Present-Apply-Review (PAR) model is most effective to address shortfalls in student learning. This is the research that guides the structure of the book. Petty's research reflects a high level of evidence.
- Research on the importance of student engagement in the learning process and the efficacy of constructivist approaches in meaning making is presented throughout Chapters 1 and 2, which supports the strategies in Chapters 3, 4, and 5. Moreover, the strategies have been used by the authors and those who have been involved in pilot versions, offering the strategies themselves as best practices via expert consensus. Similarly, the process of lesson remodeling as it is articulated in this book has also been tested and is a best practice among practitioners.
- Finally, we present compelling empirical evidence in Chapter 2 to support the efficacy of teacher learning and professional learning communities as major drivers in improving student outcomes. This suggests that, if applied judiciously, lesson remodeling can contribute to better, more effective teaching *and* learning.

Book Features

Because of its intended purpose, this book is designed for teacher convenience. Some of the important features to be aware of include the following:

- *Process diagrams* and *examples of pre- and post-remodeled lessons* offer guidance on how to approach lesson improvement and how to use the various strategies.
- Strategies *organized within the three categories of learning* offer a balance of PAR strategies to choose from when remodeling. Keep in mind, however, that many of the strategies can be adapted to fit into multiple categories.
- *Very brief and very clear instructions* demonstrate how each strategy works within the following headings for easy reference: Rationale, Ideal for, Materials, Description, and (where applicable) Cautions.

- *Reproducibles* are included for many of the strategies, as well as for use in professional learning communities.
- A *Correlation to Common Core State Standards Anchors* are available online at http://www.corwin.com/95strategies. These allow teachers to identify how strategies help them to address these important learning expectations.
- A *Professional Learning Community Guide* located in Appendix B provides suggestions that can be adapted to meet teachers' needs if they work collaboratively to remodel. The guide offers structures for PLC meetings, as well as additional resources in the form of reproducibles.

Now, it's time to remodel. Let's put our hard hats on and get to work!

Acknowledgments

Heartfelt thanks are also due to so very, very many who made the project possible and supported my work:

- Adam for consistent good advice on all things and being the best friend, *Plintock*, and partner anyone could hope for. *Stebuklas!*
- Humphrey Chimpden Earwicker, a fine canine collaborator on all my projects, though he seems to make most of his contributions entirely with his tail . . . *ir visado protingas pagalbininkas be pinigų. J'adore, mano meškiukas juodnosiukas.*
- Dr. John Portelli (*grazzi hafna*), Dr. Megan Boler, and Dr. Lennox Borel, who have inspired me so much throughout the years and who have offered me so many opportunities to learn, for which I'm eternally grateful.
- Our fantastic editor, Hudson Perigo, for her graciousness and guidance, and the entire team at Corwin who made this happen.
- Dr. Liz Coulson for always encouraging me, helping me out at a moment's notice, and being a greater inspiration than she probably realizes.
- The dozens and dozens of teachers and colleagues who offered ideas, advice, and feedback on this manuscript. It could not have evolved to this point without you.
- And last but definitely not least, my besties and immediate family, who have all supported my work, endured my unavailability, offered invaluable advice, and cut me lots of slack when I'm pressed for time, especially, but not limited to Bronė, Bob, Rob, Justine, Anne-Marie, and Wendy. *Didelis ačiū jums, mielieji!*

Laura E. Pinto
Toronto, 2011

I would like to thank the following people. First, a huge thanks to my coauthors, Laura Pinto and Laura Driscoll, for their dedication, hard work, constant support, and friendship. Second, to the class-mates and instructors in my 2008/09 cohort at Ontario Institute for Studies in Education (OISE), University of Toronto, who inspired the idea in the first place! A very important thank-you goes to Rebecca and Lindsay. "You are the reason I had the courage to get into teaching in the first place!" Finally, and most importantly, thank you to my family and friends, who have been supportive in so many ways that it would be impossible to list them all.

Stephanie Spares
Oakville, 2011

I am extremely grateful to my coauthors for all the time and effort spent on this project, without which this would not have been possible. I also wish to thank all of my friends and family for their constant support, especially Katie Waterston, Daniel Bernstein, and Beverley Driscoll.

I wish to express my deepest gratitude for the lifelong guidance of my parents, Helen and Marv Bernstein, who have helped me accomplish so much. Finally, I want to thank my husband, Brandon Driscoll, for always being there with unconditional love and the encouragement to pursue my dreams.

Laura Driscoll
Toronto, 2011

Publisher's Acknowledgments

Corwin wishes to acknowledge the following peer reviewers for their editorial insight and guidance.

Melissa Albright
Fifth-Grade Communication
Arts Teacher
Springfield Public Schools
(Wilson's Creek)
Battlefield, MO

Julie Duford
Fifth-Grade Teacher
Polson Middle School
Polson, MT

Cindy Corlett
Teacher, Building Resource
Teacher, Professional Developer
Douglas County School
District—Cimarron Middle
School
Parker, CO

About the Authors

Award-winning researcher and educator **Dr. Laura E. Pinto** is currently assistant professor of educational leadership at Niagara University and associate member of the Graduate Faculty, Department of Theory & Policy Studies in Education, University of Toronto. She has been teaching in faculties of education for the past decade and working with new and seasoned members of the teaching profession with an eye to applying evidence and promising practices to their work. Dr. Pinto began her career as a schoolteacher, which led her to write curriculum policy for the government of Ontario. Before long, she became a policy analyst and policy manager prior to commencing her doctoral studies. She is also a past president of the Ontario Business Educators' Association. She received the prestigious Canadian Governor General's Gold Medal in 2009 for her research, as well as the Odyssey Award, among other honors. She has been involved in large-scale research projects supported by sought-after Social Sciences and Humanities Research Council grants for a decade. Dr. Pinto coauthored three Canadian textbooks and related teachers' guides: *Insights* (Irwin), *Business Technology Today* (Nelson), and *Business Connections* (Prentice Hall) and authored *Curriculum Reform in Ontario: "Common Sense" Policy Processes and Democratic Possibilities* (University of Toronto Press). She has authored and coauthored dozens of articles in academic and professional journals. She has cowritten provincial curriculum policy and continues to provide advice to various governments on matters of education policy. She regularly delivers papers and workshops at scholarly and professional conferences both locally and internationally. Dr. Pinto is deeply committed to democracy in education and education for critical democracy and is particularly interested in the role of politics, policy production, and critical thinking to democracy.

Photo by BigDaddyKreativ.ca

Stephanie Spares is currently a high school business teacher at Mentor College in Port Credit, Ontario, Canada. Prior to her teaching career, Stephanie spent five years as a leader and mentor in a teen and young adults program in Oakville, Ontario, Canada. She decided to pursue teaching after a trip to Zambia with Habitat for Humanity in 2007, and she continues to participate in builds with the organization. Her first teaching position was with a public girls' school in St. Albans, Hertfordshire, England, where she taught business and economics in 2010.

Stephanie has been a member of the Ontario Business Educators Association (OBEA) since 2011 and participates in the Chartered Accountants of Ontario Teacher Colleague Program. During the school year, Stephanie is involved in leading her school's Sprott Business Competition (SBC) team and the DECA group in addition to coaching at Mentor College.

Photo by Brandon Driscoll.

Laura Driscoll is a business studies and accounting teacher with the Toronto District School Board in Toronto, Ontario, Canada. Laura has extensive experience in remodeling lessons. She has used these techniques to increase student engagement in her own classroom. The strategies included in this book have been beneficial in adapting mandated curriculum requirements for all students, including those at-risk and with special education needs.

Laura has always had a passion for both learning and helping others learn, which led her to pursue her bachelor of education degree from the Ontario Institute for Studies in Education (OISE) at the University of Toronto. She is an Ontario Certified Teacher and also a member of the Ontario Business Educators' Association (OBEA). In addition to helping coach volleyball and track and field, Laura has participated in developing curriculum resources for outside organizations and securing and implementing grants for financial literacy education at her home school. Laura enjoys traveling, skiing, camping, and biking and is an avid reader.

1

Pedagogies in Context

Why Remodel Lessons?

The purpose of this book is to apply the best practices emerging from research and theory in order to help you, the teacher, build lessons that are creative, engaging to students, and as effective as possible in facilitating the learning process.

To achieve this, you'll begin by exploring the context of what's known about pedagogies, tracing some of the major developments in learning theory and recent research to support effective lesson planning and design. By the end of Chapter 1, you should have a basis for understanding how to improve lessons.

In Chapter 2, you'll be introduced to the process of lesson remodeling and, by applying the content of this book, walk through the re-creation of several sample lessons that are connected to the Common Core State Standards for English Language Arts, Literacy in the Social Studies, and Science and Technical Subjects, as well as to the Common Core State Standards Anchors. We then invite you to do the same for your own lessons, drawing on the 95 pedagogical strategies in Chapters 3, 4, and 5 to create better, more creative, and evidence-based lessons. The payoff will be increased student engagement, and perhaps even enhanced teacher engagement, as you challenge yourself to reinvent your lessons by infusing new strategies into the learning process.

Pedagogies as a Dance to the Music of the Content

The word *pedagogy* comes from the ancient Greek *paidagogos*, the slave who took little boys to and from school. *Merriam-Webster's* defines pedagogy as "the art, science, or profession of teaching." Put in simpler terms, pedagogy is the *how* of education—what teaching/learning/instructional strategies are used. Chapters 3, 4, and 5 of this book provide you with a library of pedagogies to use.

One helpful analogy is that of the dance. Think of pedagogy as the steps in the dance, the body movements, and so on. You cannot dance knowing the steps alone; you also need music. And you need the right music for the steps (or vice versa); salsa dance steps will not work with waltz music. In our analogy, music is the content or topics taught. When you put the music and the steps together, you can dance. Similarly, when you put the pedagogy and the content together, you can teach and students can learn.

While pedagogy is defined as a discrete part of education, it does not happen in isolation from content or from educational philosophy. It influences and is influenced by content and topics (e.g., a teacher must ensure that pedagogies fit with content and topics). Educational philosophy shapes pedagogies as well, and in turn, a teacher's educational philosophy might be shaped by the pedagogies he or she uses. This is illustrated in Figure 1.1.

Figure 1.1 The What, How, and Why of Education

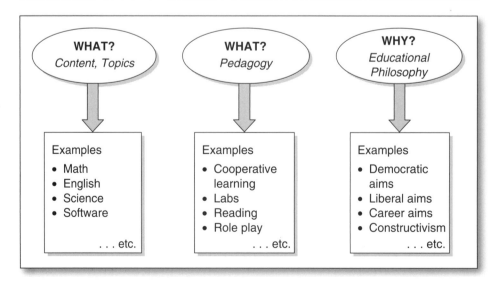

Part of your professional responsibility as a teacher is making pedagogical decisions—choosing from the countless pedagogies available and adapting them to your classroom.

There are many criteria you probably already consider—sometimes consciously, sometimes intuitively—in making pedagogical choices. These criteria might include the following:

- Appropriateness for the content or subject (e.g., in a science course, a hands-on pedagogy for students to perform experiments and experience lab activities)
- The degree to which it addresses particular learning outcomes, such as Common Core State Standards and Anchor Standards
- Age appropriateness for the grade level taught
- Evidence that the pedagogy contributes to student achievement (e.g., past experience, readings, advice from colleagues)
- Alignment with the teacher's educational philosophy or views on education (e.g., for a student-centered teaching philosophy, encouraging students to be active learners)

As you think about pedagogy, keep the following assumptions in mind:

- No two students are alike.
- No two students learn in the identical way.
- An enriched environment for one student is not necessarily enriched for another.
- In the classroom, we should teach students to think for themselves.

In the next section, you'll receive an overview of how our understandings have evolved over time.

Learning Theories Over Time

Since theorists started examining education, a number of frameworks to understand learning have come and gone. This section will provide a very brief introduction to some of the major theories and frameworks, as summarized in Figure 1.2.

To begin, let's explore the body of knowledge on teaching and learning over time. Figure 1.3 illustrates how we have gone from fairly simple cause-and-effect understandings of education to more intricate theories that address the complexities of how learners participate in the process of making meaning.

Figure 1.2	Major Theories Summarized

Behaviorism	It defines learning as a change in behavior.
	The learner is passive, responding to environmental stimuli.
	Behavior is shaped through positive or negative reinforcement immediately after a behavior, which increases the probability that the behavior will happen again.
Constructivism	Learning is an active process of constructing knowledge based on personal experiences in a specific context.
	Learners continuously test these hypotheses through social negotiation and bring past experiences and cultural factors to any situation.
	As defined by Vygotsky (1978), learning occurs within the zone of proximal development (ZPD), which is the distance between a student's ability to perform a task under adult guidance or with collaboration and the student's ability to solve the problem independently.

Figure 1.3	Pedagogical Theories Over Time

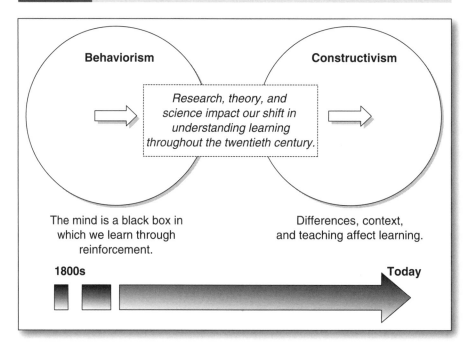

These theories also shed light on the underlying assumptions that we as teachers all hold when thinking about teaching and learning. While teachers continue to use elements of behaviorism, many of us blend it with aspects of constructivism, design-based learning, and humanism.

Much has been written about constructivist learning over the past decade, and it is certainly the predominant paradigm in contemporary educational understanding. The key underlying principle of constructivism is the assumption that understanding must be created by students rather than given to them. According to Moersch (1998), constructivism is a philosophical view on how we come to know and learn, and it can be summarized using three fundamental propositions:

1. Understanding is in our interactions with the environment.

2. Cognitive conflict or puzzlement is the stimulus for learning and determines the organization and nature of what is learned.

3. Knowledge evolves through social negotiation and through the evaluation of the viability of individual understandings. (p. 51)

Within constructivism, then, the accent is on the learner rather than the teacher. Unlike the behaviorist tradition, in which the learner is seen as passive, absorbing information transmitted by teacher, constructivism demands activity on the part of the learner. Being passive, the learner is powerless and is subject to the authority of the teacher or trainer, whose main concern is to deliver a standard curriculum and to evaluate stable underlying differences between learners.

It's worth noting that constructivism is largely attributed to John Dewey, an American philosopher, psychologist, and educational reformer. While Dewey's work from the early to mid-1900s reached far beyond education to include philosophy, democracy, and society, he had a major influence on our knowledge of learning in the present day, which he outlined in his works over several decades—*My Pedagogic Creed* (1897), *The School and Society* (1900), *The Child and the Curriculum* (1902), *Democracy and Education* (1916), and *Experience and Education* (1938). Throughout his work, Dewey argued that learners thrive in an environment where they are allowed to experience and interact with the curriculum, and all students should have the opportunity to take part in their own learning. John Dewey believed that education depended on action. Knowledge and ideas only emerged from a situation in which the learners had to draw them out of experiences that had meaning and importance to them. These situations had to occur in a social setting, such as a classroom, where students were involved in manipulating materials; therefore, a community of learners was built and knowledge was formed together within the community.

Research tends to support constructivist pedagogies as effective in deep student learning. Indeed, more recent neuroscientific research (for example, Blakemore & Choudhury, 2006; Rushton & Rushton, 2008; Tate, 2010; van Duijvenvoorde, Zanolie, Rombouts, Raijmakers, & Crone, 2008) focusing on brain development in children and adolescents further supports a movement away from teacher centeredness if we are to create environments that stimulate student learning.

It is generally accepted that teachers ought to *scaffold* learning so that students begin with learning lower-order concepts (knowledge and facts) and work their way up to higher-order skills (synthesizing, analyzing, and applying). Scaffolding means structuring learning sequentially so that topics and assessment build on one another from lower- to higher-order thinking. In practice, this means that questions on a worksheet should move from knowledge to understanding, to application, and so on. To begin scaffolding, first ask students for their prior knowledge on the topic and follow with questions moving upward from knowledge. The concept of scaffolding is derived from Vygotsky's zone of proximal development (ZPD), the difference between what a learner can do without help versus with help.

Understanding Student Centeredness in Learning

Now we will take our discussion of learning theory to a more concrete level. Consider that pedagogies are often discussed in terms of *teacher centeredness* (or teacher directed) versus *student centeredness* (or student directed)—yet another classification system used for understanding pedagogy. Generally speaking, teacher-centered approaches are associated with behaviorism, while student-centered approaches are associated with constructivist and humanist theories. Constructivism requires that the locus of responsibility for learning shifts from the teacher to the learner, who is no longer seen as passive or powerless. The learner is viewed as an individual who is active in constructing new knowledge and understanding, while the teacher is seen as a *facilitator* rather than a dictator in the process.

Also, central to constructivism is that the learner interacts with his or her environment and through that interaction gains an understanding of its features and characteristics. Learners construct their own understandings and find their own solutions to problems rather than being told what to know or do by a teacher. Learning is believed to be the result of individual mental construction in small steps where the learner matches new against given information rather than by memorization. This does *not* mean giving the learner a problem and leaving it up to him or her to figure it out. Rather, the teacher's job is to structure the path that will lead to the problem's solution—to guide the learning toward success and not leave the learner to struggle.

Both teacher- and student-centered approaches have their place in education—the challenge is to strike a balance that works for the students involved, as well as the subject matter. The table in Figure 1.4 suggests just a few examples in each category.

The work of Edgar Dale (1969) during the 1960s argues that student-centered learning results in greater learning and retention. His *Cone of Experience* (see Figure 1.5) summarizes his theory and research and is consistent with the constructivist perspective that, if students are to learn, they must be actively engaged in the process.

The PAR Model: Applying Evidence to Practice

Research suggests that students only retain 20% of what they learn (Gardiner, 1998). How much do you remember from your high school courses? Why?

Geoff Petty's (2009) extensive research into effective teaching suggests that the Present-Apply-Review (PAR) model is the most effective (see Figure 1.6). This is the framework that guides this book and the process of lesson remodeling that we offer in Chapter 2.

In his research, Petty (2009) found that optimal learning occurs when no more than 35% of instructional time is spent on the presentation of

| Figure 1.4 | Examples of Teacher- and Student-Centered Pedagogies |

Teacher-Centered/Directed Pedagogies (Instructional Strategies)	Student-Centered Pedagogies (Learning Strategies)
Lecture	Cooperative learning
Readings	Authentic and project-based learning
Demonstration	Cooperative learning (role play, simulation, discussion, dramatization, concept maps, mind maps, debates, seminars, interviews, in-basket exercises)
Socratic	
Case studies	
Field trips	
Guest speakers	
Drill and practice	
Worksheets	

Figure 1.5   The Cone of Experience

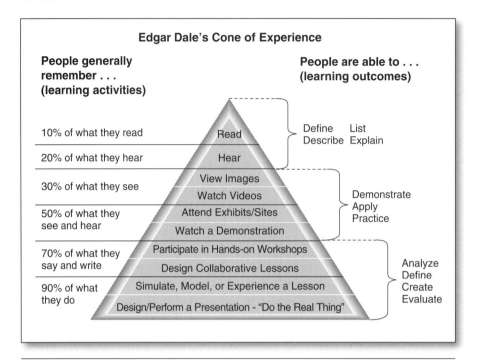

Source: Creative Commons (http://en.wikipedia.org/wiki/File:Cone_of_learning_
export_11x17.png)

Figure 1.6   The PAR Model

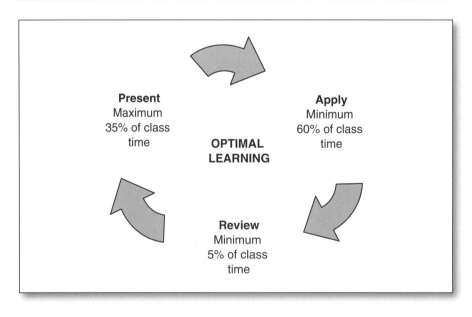

new material, at least 60% of instructional time allows students to actively apply concepts, and no less than 5% of instructional time is spent on reviewing learning or material.

When we layer this evidence with what we know about effective instruction, we can conclude the following:

- Relatively little time (no more than about one-third) should be spent on presenting new content, and the presentation of new content should avoid teacher centeredness whenever possible.
- The majority of instructional time should be spent allowing students to apply new concepts and ideas through active learning. Students' active application should be structured and carefully thought out by teachers to ensure that students master learning expectations or outcomes. In addition, opportunities to apply should be varied to address learner difference and to engage students through well-designed and novel experiences.
- Some review is necessary for closure, but the time spent on review should not be excessive, though no less than 5% of instructional time. As with presenting and applying, teachers must strive to offer students meaningful opportunities for review, which are student centered, varied, and engaging.

Applying PAR also involves differentiating instruction for your students. Some have used the analogy of an orchestra to illustrate the concept of differentiated instruction. In this analogy, the teacher is the conductor. The conductor has a variety of musicians playing simultaneously—each one has a different strength and a different way of playing the song based on his or her instrument. Thus, the conductor has to ensure that everyone in the orchestra knows the same song but knows it in different ways.

In differentiated instruction, the teacher applies the same learning expectations to all students (the song in our analogy), but how students in the class experience or demonstrate those learning expectations will vary depending on their learning styles, preferences, needs, and strengths.

Essentially, there are four ways to differentiate:

1. Differentiating content/topic, which might involve allowing students to do independent projects based on their interests, curiosities, or strengths; varying an assignment or activity. For example, in a

marketing class, you might have students study advertising campaigns; however, allow students to select which industry interests them in order to promote a higher level of engagement.

2. Differentiating process/activities, which would entail varied lesson plans so that different students have unique opportunities to learn simultaneously. Suppose you were having students research a particular topic. You might allow some students to work independently in the lab to conduct online research. Some might work in small groups in the classroom, while others might venture out into the community to conduct interviews with community members.

3. Differentiating product, which might involve different assignments or performance tasks. However, regardless of the type of assignment, all students would be assessed with the same learning expectations. For instance, at the end of a unit, you might give students the option of creating a webpage, a PowerPoint presentation, or an essay to showcase their understanding of a topic. Thus, the topic or content would be the same, but the way it is presented would be differentiated. By differentiating the product, you might also allow highly motivated students to create a more complicated product, and those struggling, a less elaborate product. Again, the learning expectations would remain the same; how those expectations take shape would be different.

4. Differentiating by manipulating the environment and/or accommodating individual learning styles. Of the four, this is the most complicated way to differentiate learning, though it can go hand in hand with the other three. You might manipulate the environment to address multiple intelligences; thus, process/activities are also differentiated. You might accommodate individual learning styles by differentiating the product students create.

This book helps you to achieve that type of differentiation by applying Petty's research to meet the needs of all learners. By flipping through the many strategies in Chapters 3, 4, and 5, you will have a wealth of ideas at your fingertips that you can vary to meet the needs of all learners while engaging them in order to promote student success.

The strategies in this book are fully aligned to the Common Core State Standards for English and Language Arts, Literacy in the Social Studies, and Science and Technical Subjects (see the online correlations at http://www.corwin.com/95strategies). This allows you to select evidence-based instruction while working toward meeting the expectations laid out in the anchors.

Chapter Conclusion

The body of knowledge about what works in education has evolved over time. We now know that student achievement requires good teaching that is student centered, differentiated, and varied to meet multiple learning needs and preferences and that follows a Present-Apply-Review format.

In the next chapter, you will be introduced to the process of lesson remodeling, which will guide you through the process of taking an existing lesson and retrofitting it by applying evidence-informed promising practices. Chapters 3, 4, and 5 provide you with the pedagogical *steps and moves* that you can set to the *music* of your subject discipline to enhance your teaching with the needs of your students in mind.

2

Lesson Remodeling

How to Remodel Lessons

 Chapter 1 provided you with a foundation for applying evidence to improve lesson planning within the Present-Apply-Review (PAR) sequence. In this chapter, we lay out a framework for remodeling lessons by taking an existing lesson and applying new, student-centered practices to improve the level of student engagement and efficacy of the learning process.

As professionals, we must constantly reflect on our work with the intent of continuous improvement. This can help us bridge the transition from *habitual practice* to *intelligent practice* or move us from active knowing to cognitive knowing (van Manen, 1995). In other words, we can get stuck in our usual, habitual ways of teaching, but reflection can guide us into improved practice through thorough examination of our habits and move us toward new and innovative ways of approaching our work. There are many ways to approach professional reflection. John Smyth (1994) reminds us that continual reflection on classroom practice can be accomplished by asking difficult questions of our own teaching (see Figure 2.1). He proposes four themes we ought to pose when considering our work in the classroom:

- Describe: What do I do as a teacher?
- Inform: What does this mean to my students?

- Confront: How did I come to approach my work this way?
- Reconstruct: How might I do things differently?

These questions constitute a good tool to form the basis of lesson remodeling activities. They serve as a disruption to our typical sequence of planning and doing, causing us to reconsider our classroom practice and move away from habitual teaching. As such, Smyth invites practitioners in the classroom to describe what it is they do with a view to greater understanding.

Figure 2.1 Elaborating on Smyth's Model for Critical Reflection

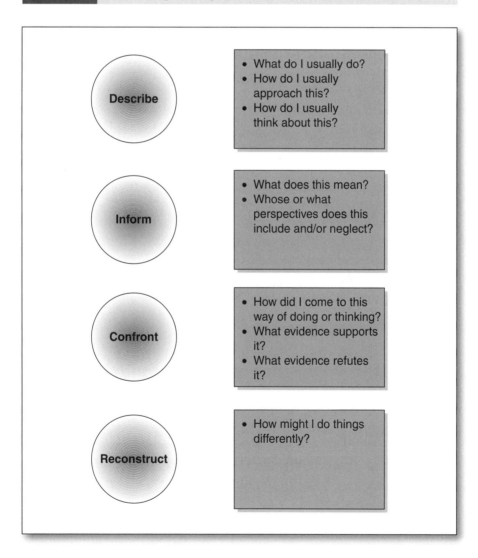

Lesson Remodeling as Reflective Practice

But how can you apply this reflective practice to your teaching? We recommend the process of lesson remodeling. Think about a remodeling project you've been involved in—a house, a condo, a garage, or maybe your school. How did you approach it? What did you keep? What did you change? How did you make those decisions?

Lesson remodeling takes the basic premises of any remodeling process reflected in these questions but applies it to your work in the classroom.

In the sections that follow, we'll walk you through an approach to lesson remodeling that you can apply to your own teaching. Get your hard hat out, and roll up your sleeves as we begin the journey.

Lesson Remodeling Explained

The concept for lesson remodeling has been pioneered by the Critical Thinking Community with groups of teachers within professional learning communities. In essence, teachers trade lessons to improve them for a particular purpose (to incorporate critical thinking). This chapter uses the framework for lesson remodeling but focuses on making lessons more student centered and grounded in evidence for greater efficacy in the learning process.

Here, we apply Geoff Petty's research on structuring lessons through PAR in order to maximize student learning and engagement. By remodeling your own lessons to PAR and applying the instructional variety in Chapters 3, 4, and 5, the results are better, more engaging, and more varied lessons to meet the needs of many learners.

Steps in the Process of Lesson Remodeling

Just like a remodeling project in your home or school, lesson remodeling begins with what is already there. You typically start with an existing lesson—one that probably has its own strengths—but then you look to see how you can improve it. You might approach this by yourself or with other teachers who can remodel each other's lessons.

That's when you put on the hard hat and pull out your tool kit. You use what you have available in that tool kit to tweak, improve, and put a fresh, new face on a lesson. Figure 2.2 provides a graphic of the four steps involved in remodeling:

1. Review the original lesson and identify the sections that would be present, apply, and review. Analyze the proportion of time spent on each, and identify changes necessary in order to address evidence-based practice (see Geoff Petty's breakdown in Figure 1.6 on page 8 of this book).

2. Identify the assessment or performance task and assess the degree to which it
   - addresses the lesson's stated outcomes/learning expectations in a way that would allow for evidence of mastery of the expectations and
   - addresses student centeredness, which would allow the learner to actively participate in the content.

3. Make note of any of the following features of the original lesson:
   - Degree to which each part of the lesson is teacher centered versus student centered
   - Degree to which the lesson offers variety in the types of pedagogies employed
   - Review the steps leading up to the performance task or assessment. Do they lead the student toward mastery?

4. Remodel the lesson by
   - updating the assessment or performance task if necessary;
   - flipping through Chapters 3, 4, and 5 of this book to identify alternate approaches to teaching/learning and noting those that are most appropriate; and
   - updating the lesson accordingly.

To assist you in getting a handle on this process, we have remodeled several lessons for you, along with explanations, in Examples 1 through 5 beginning on page 18. Review them and then try to remodel a lesson of your own or a colleague's lesson.

Integrating Common Core State Standards

The Common Core State Standards provide a consistent, clear understanding of what students are expected to learn, defining the knowledge and skills students should have within their K–12 education in addition to the individual state standards in each subject area. Each of the pedagogies in the tool kit is aligned to Grade 6 to 12

| Figure 2.2 | The Lesson Remodeling Process |

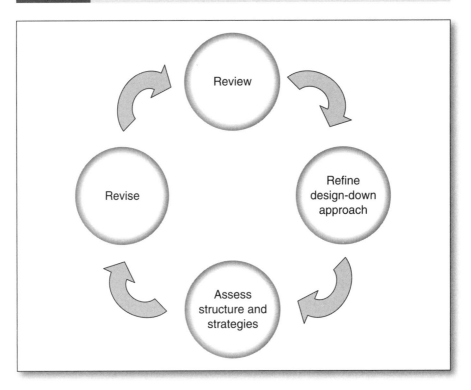

Common Core State Standards Anchors for English Language Arts and Literacy in History/Social Studies, Science, and Technical Subjects. The specific connections are summarized online at http://www.corwin.com/95strategies. Many of the pedagogies can also be applied in conjunction with Mathematics Common Core State Standards at all levels, particularly with respect to literacy building and collaborative work within the mathematics curriculum.

Applying Design-Down or Backward Planning

Whereas the paradigms of lesson planning linked assessment to resources, units, and themes, the new paradigm organizes assessment and instruction to clearly stated expectations. Movement toward the new paradigm is marked by *design-down* or *backward* planning (McTighe & Thomas, 2003), which involves starting instructional design with expectations to be evaluated, and then, identifying what student performance or activities will demonstrate mastery of those expectations. Next, the assessment tool or method is selected, followed by the design of a lesson or activity around that assessment tool or method. Finally, the new paradigm represents the use of a variety of assessment strategies, as well as varied learning strategies. This process is illustrated in Figure 2.3.

Figure 2.3 Design-Down or Backward Planning

1. Expectations
   - Determine what learning expectations or outcomes students will achieve, at both the state and district levels, and in terms of the Common Core State Standards.

⇩

2. Assessment/Evaluation Strategies
   - Determine the best way to evaluate whether students demonstrate their mastery of the learning expectations or outcomes.

⇩

3. Teaching/Learning Strategies
   - Determine the best teaching/learning strategies that will meet the objectives *and* prepare students to succeed in the assessment/evaluation strategies chosen, such as those outlined in Chapters 3, 4, and 5 of this book.

⇩

4. Topic/Theme/Resources
   - Identify the topic, theme, and resources that are required for the teaching/learning strategies selected.
   - Obtain or create the resources identified and plan the lesson accordingly.

This approach to planning for student learning also ensures that assessments are carefully chosen and aligned to learning expectations or outcomes and that the lesson itself is scaffolded in a way that allows students to practice the subtasks necessary for mastery of the knowledge and skills assessed, consistent with Common Core State Standards recommendations. In this way, the entire lesson sets the student up to succeed, as emphasized in the work of Jay McTighe and Ronald Thomas (2003), and the lesson not only addresses assessment *of* learning but also assessment *for* learning (Stiggins, 2005).

Effective assessment strategies ought to

- address both what students learn and how well they learn;
- be based both on the categories of knowledge and skills and on the achievement level descriptions given in the achievement chart that appears in the curriculum policy document for each discipline;
- be varied in nature, administered over a period of time, and designed to provide opportunities for students to demonstrate the full range of their learning;
- be appropriate for the learning activities used, the purposes of instruction, and the needs and experiences of the students;
- be fair to all students;

- accommodate the needs of exceptional students consistent with the strategies outlined in their Individual Education Plan;
- accommodate the needs of students who are learning the language of instruction;
- ensure that each student is given clear directions for improvement;
- promote students' ability to assess their own learning and to set specific goals;
- include the use of samples of students' work that provide evidence of their achievement; and
- be communicated clearly to students and parents at the beginning of the course and at other appropriate points throughout the course.

Examples of Remodeled Lessons

Now that you've learned about the process and theoretical foundations of remodeling, you're probably wondering how it looks in action. In the subsections that follow, you can view five remodeled lessons for various grade levels and subject areas. Note that each one provides a side-by-side comparison of the original and remodeled lesson. A full explanation of the rationale behind the changes follows. While these examples offer extensive remodeling, keep in mind that the extremes are for explanatory purposes. More than likely, you will find that you need only tweak your lessons here and there, not necessarily make extensive changes as we have shown.

Example 1: Lesson Remodeling, Middle School History

Subject: Grade 6 Social Studies

Expectations/Outcomes

- The student understands important issues, events, and individuals of the 20th century in the United States.
  - o Analyze various issues and events of the 20th century such as urbanization, industrialization, increased use of oil and gas, world wars, and the Great Depression.
  - o Identify the accomplishments of notable individuals such as Carrie Chapman Catt, Dwight Eisenhower, Martin Luther King, Jr., Rosa Parks, Colin Powell, and Franklin D. Roosevelt who have made contributions to society in the areas of civil rights, women's rights, military actions, and politics.
- The student communicates in written, oral, and visual forms.
- The student uses problem-solving and decision-making skills, working independently and with others, in a variety of settings.

Common Core State Standards

SL.6.1. Engage effectively in a range of collaborative discussions (one-on-one, in groups, and teacher-led) with diverse partners on grade 6 topics, texts, and issues, building on others' ideas and expressing their own clearly.

- Come to discussions prepared, having read or studied required material; explicitly draw on that preparation by referring to evidence on the topic, text, or issue to probe and reflect on ideas under discussion.
- Follow rules for collegial discussions, set specific goals and deadlines, and define individual roles as needed.
- Pose and respond to specific questions with elaboration and detail by making comments that contribute to the topic, text, or issue under discussion.
- Review the key ideas expressed and demonstrate understanding of multiple perspectives through reflection and paraphrasing.

SL.6.2. Interpret information presented in diverse media and formats (e.g., visually, quantitatively, orally) and explain how it contributes to a topic, text, or issue under study.

W.6.2. Write informative/explanatory texts to examine a topic and convey ideas, concepts, and information through the selection, organization, and analysis of relevant content. Introduce a topic; organize ideas, concepts, and information, using strategies such as definition, classification, comparison/contrast, and cause/effect; include formatting (e.g., headings), graphics (e.g., charts, tables), and multimedia when useful to aiding comprehension.

- Develop the topic with relevant facts, definitions, concrete details, quotations, or other information and examples.
- Use appropriate transitions to clarify the relationships among ideas and concepts.
- Use precise language and domain-specific vocabulary to inform about or explain the topic.

W.6.7. Conduct short research projects to answer a question, drawing on several sources and refocusing the inquiry when appropriate.

Original Lesson	Remodeled Lesson
Assessment or Performance Task • Completion of questions from textbook • Quiz (each Monday)	Assessment or Performance Task • Completion of an exhibit for a class Virtual Museum (see Strategy 67 on page 124)
Present Strategies • Take up previous day's homework. • Using PowerPoint, provide the class with an overview of the period as well as some general information about the realities of the Great Depression. • Using Socratic questioning, the teacher asks a series of questions to check for understanding and analysis of students' mastery of issues and events in the Great Depression.	Present Strategies • Use two rounds of Hot Potato (see Strategy 5 on page 38) to (1) have students share what they know about how the economy affects families, and (2) have students share what they know about the Great Depression.

(Continued)

(Continued)

Apply Strategies	Apply Strategies

• Show excerpts from the 1998 miniseries *The Great Depression*, available online, to give students a visual perspective on the era.
• Students have the remainder of the period to get started on questions 1–8 (p. 239 of textbook).
	• Explain that students will learn about the Great Depression by creating a class Virtual Museum (see Strategy 67 on page 124). As a group, generate criteria about what makes an effective museum exhibit. These criteria will be translated into the assessment for the task.
	• The following exhibit topics will be assigned to groups of students:
	  o Politics
	  o The economic situation
	  o Religious life
	  o Immigration
	  o Scientific advances and changes
	  o The job market
	• Students will be given one class to research in the library and lab and one class to produce their exhibit. The teacher will assemble all exhibits onto a DVD using web authoring software so that each student has a copy to keep.

Review Strategies	Review Strategies
• As homework, students complete a crossword puzzle on key themes from the Great Depression. • At the beginning of next class, take up homework and the textbook questions.	• As a class, visit the Virtual Museum, and as a large group, create a Did Well/Do Better assessment of the project as a whole. • Based on the contents of the Virtual Museum, table groups create a Wired Knowledge (see Strategy 48 on page 101) of the era based on what they learned, which will be displayed in the classroom.

Example 1 Explanation

The original lesson was highly teacher centered and relied on independent work largely driven by the textbook, although there was an effort to integrate media via the use of video.

In the remodeled lesson, students begin by considering their prior knowledge or understanding, which may be from textbook readings, as well as knowledge from other sources outside of school. This also provides the teacher with some diagnostic assessment. Next, students actively engage in researching and creating museum exhibits, which allows for exploration and construction of knowledge as a group. As well, since the exhibits can potentially take a variety of forms (video, audio, visual, written), there is potential for all students to demonstrate their understanding by using their own strengths. Many will be further engaged by the use of technology.

Finally, the Review strategies in the remodeled lesson allow students to celebrate their successes while learning from peers' research. A final use of the Wired Knowledge strategy (see Strategy 48 on page 101) allows the teacher to ensure mastery of understanding about the Great Depression in table groups.

Example 2: Lesson Remodeling, Middle School (English and Media Studies)

Subject: Grade 7 English/Media Studies

Expectations/Outcomes

- Demonstrate an understanding of a variety of media texts.
- Explain how both simple and complex media texts are created to suit particular purposes and audiences (e.g., both the feature articles and the advertisements in a women's fashion magazine are designed to appeal to—and influence—women's sense of fashion and beauty and to promote sales; a webpage about skateboarding has both video clips that feature new and challenging jumps and links to advertisers promoting the latest equipment).

Common Core State Standards

RI.7.4. Determine the meaning of words and phrases as they are used in a text, including figurative, connotative, and technical meanings; analyze the impact of a specific word choice on meaning and tone.

RI.7.5. Analyze the structure an author uses to organize a text, including how the major sections contribute to the whole and to the development of the ideas.

RI.7.7. Compare and contrast a text to an audio, video, or multimedia version of the text analyzing each medium's portrayal of the subject (e.g., how the delivery of a speech affects the impact of the words).

RI.7.8. Trace and evaluate the argument and specific claims in a text, assessing whether the reasoning is sound and the evidence is relevant and sufficient to support the claims.

Original Lesson	Remodeled Lesson
Assessment or Performance Task	Assessment or Performance Task
Create an ad for a fashion magazine or a storyboard for a fashion-related video.	Create a set of correspondence that explores media texts' dual purposes.
Present Strategies	Present Strategies
Show the Dove Campaign for Real Beauty video (online) and ask students the following: • Who is the audience? How do you know? • What is the message that the video tries to send? • What is the purpose of this video?	Show the Dove Campaign for Real Beauty video (online) with guided prompts for students to focus on • Intended audience • Purpose • Examples of arguments in the video

(Continued)

(Continued)

• Why would Dove create a video like this?
• Who is the owner of Dove?
• How does this message/video conform to or contradict Unilever's overall product line?
• How does this compare with other advertising for beauty and fashion?
	• After viewing, students individually complete an I See, I Think, Therefore (see adapted Strategy 28 on page 67) analysis of what they saw.
	• As a large group, discuss the following:
	  o How the video challenges different approaches to beauty and fashion
	  o Why Unilever would produce this
	  o How it compares with Unilever's other products and advertisements
	  o Examples of other media texts and topics that parallel or contradict this

Apply Strategies After viewing and discussing the Dove video, students create an ad for a fashion magazine or a storyboard for a fashion-related video.	**Apply Strategies** In pairs, students select a teacher-approved topic dealing with media texts that are created to suit particular purposes and audiences. Using You've Got Mail (see Strategy 27 on page 66), they create sets of correspondence to convey the two sides of the issue, with attention to controversy. The correspondence should be a combination of cards, letters, or other forms.
Review Strategies Students share their work by having a few volunteers showcasing their creations before the teacher collects them for assessment.	**Review Strategies** Three groups combine and review each other's correspondence. The newly formed groups each create a Mind Map (see Strategy 76 on page 138) on chart paper to summarize their conclusion.

Example 2 Explanation

In the original lesson, the assessment was not aligned to the expectations, so it was updated in the remodeled lesson. The video is an excellent foundation for the exercise, but in the original lesson, students watched passively. Strategies were incorporated in the remodeled lesson to involve them in meaning making and to prepare them for the Apply strategies.

In the remodeled lesson, students work in pairs during the Apply strategy to create correspondence using You've Got Mail (see Strategy 27 on page 66). This allows them to interact deeply with the content and offers them choice in what theme they want to explore related to the issue of media texts that were created to suit particular purposes and audiences. Since students take opposing sides, they will be gaining critical thinking skills while making sense of a controversial issue. Finally, three pairs of students converge for the Review strategy, look at each other's work, and summarize their learning by creating a collective Mind Map (see Strategy 76 on page 138) to conclude their learning.

Example 3: Lesson Remodeling, High School (English and Computers)

Course: Grade 9 Information and Communication Technology in Business or English

---

Expectations/Outcomes

- Use word processing software to create common business documents.
- Use word processing software to produce properly structured and formatted business documents (e.g., letter, memo, report, résumé).
- Compose letters that follow an appropriate format with appropriate content.

Common Core Case Standards

W.9-10.2. Write informative/explanatory texts to examine and convey complex ideas, concepts, and information clearly and accurately through the effective selection, organization, and analysis of content.

W.9-10.5. Develop and strengthen writing as needed by planning, revising, editing, rewriting, or trying a new approach, focusing on addressing what is most significant for a specific purpose and audience.

W.9-10.6. Use technology, including the Internet, to produce, publish, and update individual or shared writing products, taking advantage of technology's capacity to link to other information and to display information flexibly and dynamically.

Original Lesson	**Remodeled Lesson**
Assessment or Performance Task	Assessment or Performance Task
Create a business letter to express either customer satisfaction or dissatisfaction based on a recent personal experience.	Create a business letter to express either customer satisfaction or dissatisfaction based on a recent personal experience at a store or with a product.
Present Strategies	Present Strategies
Demonstrate how to use the indent features in MS Word on a projector while students follow along, doing the same things. Show an example of a business letter on a projector and explain how to write one.	In groups of four, students receive four different business letters. Using a modified placement (see Strategy 30, Placemat, on page 70), students will identify 1. Parts of a business letter common to all the examples 2. Contents of paragraphs (topics, sequence)

(Continued)

(Continued)

	3. Criteria for good letters (one letter has several mistakes to help them develop criteria)
	Once groups have finished, as a class, summarize the findings.
	Distribute the business letter rubric and a cheat sheet explaining how to use indenting in MS Word. Go over the details of the assignment with the class to ensure understanding.
Apply Strategies	Apply Strategies
Students write letters for the remainder of the period. Teacher circulates to assess work and assist if needed.	Students write letters for 45 minutes. Teacher circulates to assess work and assist if needed.
Review Strategies	Review Strategies
Teacher asks for three volunteers to read their letters. Collect letters for assessment.	In pairs, students peer edit letters, referring to the summary of criteria and parts of a letter, as well as the rubric. Students revise their work, handing in both the peer feedback and the final copy (see Strategy 72, Peer Edit, on page 132).

Example 3 Explanation

The original lesson relied on teacher-centered pedagogies to involve students in the process of learning to write a business letter. The teacher presented and demonstrated, and the students copied what they knew.

In the remodeled lesson, the Present activity allowed students to construct meaning by viewing examples. This represents a more student-centered approach through which small groups create a body of knowledge by exploration.

The Apply section of the lesson was not changed significantly, though students are able to draw on constructed knowledge rather than teacher-delivered knowledge.

Finally, the Review section changed significantly. Rather than a teacher-led summary that would have allowed only a handful of students to participate, the students were provided with a peer editing opportunity, which allowed them to work in small groups to learn from one another's products and to offer constructive feedback to one another. In this way, all students in the class actively participate in the Review.

Example 4: Lesson Remodeling, Visual Art

Subject: Grade 10 Art

Expectations/Outcomes

- VA.912.C.1.1. Integrate curiosity, range of interests, attentiveness, complexity, and artistic intention in the art-making process to demonstrate self-expression.
- VA.A.1.4.1. Use three-dimensional media, techniques, tools, and processes to communicate an idea or concept based on research, environment, personal experience, observation, or imagination.
- VA.A.1.4.4. Use effective control of media, techniques, and tools when communicating an idea in three-dimensional works of art.

Common Core State Standards

SL.9-10.1. Initiate and participate effectively in a range of collaborative discussions (one-on-one, in groups, and teacher-led) with diverse partners on grades 9–10 topics, texts, and issues, building on others' ideas and expressing their own clearly and persuasively.

Original Lesson	Remodeled Lesson
Assessment or Performance Task Students create a bas relief sculpture.	
Present Strategies <ul><li>The teacher shows students various pictures of bas relief sculptures either using an LCD projector or by posting large pictures on the board. Examples include coins, buildings, and items from online museum holdings.</li><li>The teacher provides a short explanation of the sculptural technique. Explain that students will be making their own bas relief sculptures. Review the steps of the process and the materials needed and show students a model of the finished product created by the teacher. Leave examples on the board or projector so that students can refer to them.</li></ul>	Present Strategies <ul><li>Students participate in an online Scavenger Hunt (see Strategy 64 on page 117) in groups of three. While usually a Scavenger Hunt would be an Apply strategy, in this case we adapted it for exploration of a new topic as a Present strategy. The objectives of the Scavenger Hunt are to locate examples of bas relief sculptures in (1) art museums and (2) the real world. Students will be given a list of websites to visit to ensure that they are able to find the examples.</li><li>Once the Scavenger Hunt is complete, students complete a Graffiti activity (see Strategy 6 on page 39 of this book) based on their responses. Graffiti sheets at their table groups will have the following headings:<ul><li>What are bas relief sculptures?</li><li>Examples of bas relief sculptures</li><li>Techniques and effects a bas relief includes</li><li>Ways to create texture in our bas reliefs, including materials we can use</li><li>Ways to create strength in our bas reliefs</li></ul></li></ul>

(Continued)

(Continued)

Apply Strategies	Apply Strategies
• All materials needed to construct sculptures (cardboard, glue, tape, scissors, pencils, etc.) will be on students' desks in advance. • Explain that on Day 1 of the activity, students will only cut out cardboard bone shapes and stick them to the base with tape. • On Day 2, students will apply glue and cover their sculptures with sand.	• The teacher explains the evaluation criteria for a bas relief sculpture and makes the materials available to students. • The teacher circulates while students complete the first phase, creation of the base of the bas relief sculpture, which will dry overnight. • On the second day, students apply glue and coat the sculptures with sand.
Review Strategies	Review Strategies
• Students shake off all the sand from their sculptures and submit them to the teacher for assessment.	• Students shake off all the sand from their sculptures and put them on display around the classroom for a Gallery Walk (see Strategy 68 on page 127). Feedback will be based on the stars and stairs method, wherein a star is something that the students liked about their peer's sculpture, and a stair is something that they feel their peer needs to improve on.

Example 4 Explanation

While the original lesson has a strong, student-centered component in completing the sculpture, the Present and Review strategies are highly teacher centered. The remodeled lesson engages students in the Present component by allowing them to actively investigate examples of bas relief sculptures in different contexts instead of teacher-presented examples. In addition, they build on their online investigation by making sense, drawing conclusions, and thinking creatively about how one might go about the construction of bas relief sculptures. The result is that they become more active in the process rather than simply (and possibly mindlessly) following rigid instructions. The Apply section of the lesson was remodeled slightly to involve students in the process a bit more and to ensure that they know the expectations of their projects. Finally, by displaying their work in a Gallery Walk, students are engaged in critical reflection about their own and their peers' work before teacher evaluation.

Example 5: Lesson Remodeling, High School (Science)

Course: Grade 11 Science

Expectations/Outcomes

- Identify and describe a variety of careers related to the fields of science under study and identify scientists who have made contributions to those fields.
- Identify scientists, including those who have made a contribution to the fields of science under study.

Common Core State Standards

SL.11-12.1. Initiate and participate effectively in a range of collaborative discussions (one-on-one, in groups, and teacher-led) with diverse partners on grades 11–12 topics, texts, and issues, building on others' ideas and expressing their own clearly and persuasively.

- Come to discussions prepared, having read and researched material under study; explicitly draw on that preparation by referring to evidence from texts and other research on the topic or issue to stimulate a thoughtful, well-reasoned exchange of ideas.
- Work with peers to promote civil, democratic discussions and decision-making, set clear goals and deadlines, and establish individual roles as needed.
- Propel conversations by posing and responding to questions that probe reasoning and evidence; ensure a hearing for a full range of positions on a topic or issue; clarify, verify, or challenge ideas and conclusions; and promote divergent and creative perspectives.
- Respond thoughtfully to diverse perspectives; synthesize comments, claims, and evidence made on all sides of an issue; resolve contradictions when possible; and determine what additional information or research is required to deepen the investigation or complete the task.

SL.11-12.2. Integrate multiple sources of information presented in diverse formats and media (e.g., visually, quantitatively, orally) in order to make informed decisions and solve problems, evaluating the credibility and accuracy of each source and noting any discrepancies among the data.

SL.11-12.4. Present information, findings, and supporting evidence, conveying a clear and distinct perspective, such that listeners can follow the line of reasoning, alternative or opposing perspectives are addressed, and the organization, development, substance, and style are appropriate to purpose, audience, and a range of formal and informal tasks.

SL.11-12.5. Make strategic use of digital media (e.g., textual, graphical, audio, visual, and interactive elements) in presentations to enhance understanding of findings, reasoning, and evidence and to add interest.

Original Lesson	Remodeled Lesson
Assessment or Performance Task	Assessment or Performance Task
Written report on one prominent scientist with a presentation component	Trading cards on prominent scientists

(Continued)

(Continued)

Present Strategies	Present Strategies
Students view a video (from the textbook package) that shows the accomplishments of prominent scientists.	Students view a video (from the textbook package) that shows the accomplishments of prominent scientists. After viewing, students individually complete an I See, I Think, Therefore (see adapted Strategy 28 on page 67) analysis of what they saw.
Apply Strategies	Apply Strategies
Students have one period in the library to conduct research in the computer lab in order to write a brief (one to two pages) report on a scientist and prepare a 5-minute oral presentation for the class. They have three additional days to complete their report as homework. A list is provided for them to choose a scientist, or they can select their own (not from the list) as long as it's approved by the teacher.	Prompt the class as a group to identify the components of cards that showcase athletes (e.g., baseball cards, hockey cards). Generate a list on the board of the types of information on the front and back of these types of cards.
	Ask students to identify parallel categories of information that would be relevant for scientists (for example, education, major discoveries or accomplishments, things they wrote, etc.).
	Explain that students are to create Trading Cards (see Strategy 52 on page 105) for an assigned scientist using the class-generated criteria. One side should have a photo or visual while the other side is informational. Provide students with dimensions for the final product and an evaluation rubric in advance.
	Allow ample time in the library and computer lab for students to complete this task.
	Optional: Add a Peer Edit (see Strategy 72 on page 132) phase before cards are finalized.
Review Strategies	Review Strategies
Students present their reports (5 minutes or less) to the class. The teacher assesses their work using a presentation rubric.	As a class, play a game of Who or What Am I? (see Strategy 46 on page 99) in which students present a few key facts about their scientist, and others try to guess who the card represents. While Who or What Am I? is usually an Apply strategy, here we included it as a Review strategy to bring closure to the activity.
	Allow a Gallery Walk (see Strategy 68 on page 127) to display and share information as a final stage to this lesson.

Example 5 Explanation

In the original lesson, the Present strategy involves students viewing a video. While a video offers an alternative to a lecture-based introduction, it remains a passive medium for learning and, especially without guided viewing, serves to potentially disengage students. The remodeled Present strategy invites students to make sense of the video using the I See, I Think, Therefore (see adapted Strategy 28 on page 67) format.

In the remodeled lesson, students perform research in the Apply task similar to the original, but they organize the information in a novel way—as Trading Cards (see Strategy 52 on page 105). High school students are particularly skilled at creating professional-looking and well-researched trading cards.

Finally, the Review strategy is designed to have students learn from each other's research, and the use of a game (see Strategy 46: Who or What Am I? on page 99) makes this more engaging than a straight, informational presentation, as there is suspense and competition involved.

Collaborative Lesson Remodeling in Professional Learning Communities

In a 1995 interview, Peter Senge, noted organizational theorist and author of *The Learning Organization*, proposed that, to transform schools into learning organizations, he would start by finding committed and passionate teachers who are interested in doing things differently and get them talking to one another (O'Neil, 1995).

Today, less than two decades later, collaborative learning among teachers in the form of professional learning communities (PLCs) has increased in popularity, and its success in contributing to student outcomes has been well documented. A PLC is a collaborative learning structure in which professionals who work in the same field share and exchange knowledge toward a common learning goal. PLCs can be formal or informal; they can be face-to-face or use information and communication technologies to connect their members. Among teachers, PLCs are increasingly popular. Indeed, there's a clear link between teachers' collaborative learning and student learning in the classroom—well-developed PLCs tend to have a positive impact on both teaching practice and student achievement

(Vescio, Ross, & Adams, 2008). As a means for teachers to work toward the shared purpose of improved student learning, PLCs offer an environment where the teacher-as-adult-learner can self-initiate improvement in concert with peers.

Lesson remodeling is a structured activity that embraces adult learning principles, since teachers engage in active reflection on their daily work with the goal of revision and improvement. While, as we've shown in this chapter, remodeling can be done individually, collaborative remodeling offers the benefit of a fresh pair of eyes that can offer an entirely new perspective. The social context of professional exchange, then, offers a way for remodeling to be especially productive; moreover, job-embedded collaborative learning has been shown to be especially effective (Wood & Killian, 1998).

To remodel lessons as a PLC, consider the following:

- Working with teachers in your school or across your district and across different subject and grade levels. By having a diverse group of teachers, unique perspectives may contribute to more creative problem solving. While PLCs can operate well in a face-to-face format, the use of a wiki or other online, collaborative tool can be highly effective as well.
- Establishing, at the beginning of the school year, a schedule for the PLC to meet and share their lesson plans (for example, twice per term). All participants must bring lesson plans to share with peers, and all must commit to providing honest, fair-minded feedback to other members of the group.
- Having a framework to guide your work, such as John Smyth's framework for critical reflection discussed earlier in this chapter and pictured in Figure 2.1.
- Creating criteria as a group against which to analyze lessons. It may be the criteria laid out in Chapter 1 of this book, or you may wish to expand the criteria further to address local or subject-specific needs.

While the configurations of and tasks within a PLC can vary, Appendix B offers a guide to structure meetings and to approach collaborative remodeling. We invite you to consider how you can adapt these suggestions in working with your peers.

By engaging in lesson remodeling, teachers reflect on their own work while offering feedback to peers. Although this is an extremely valuable learning process, bear in mind that giving and receiving feedback can be delicate and sometimes uncomfortable. Remember the following:

- Maintain an environment of mutual respect, caring, integrity, and truthfulness. In the early stages of a PLC, the group should consider establishing these sorts of shared values formally.
- Critique the lesson and not the individual when remodeling.
- When offering feedback, balance positive and negative comments.
- When receiving feedback, keep in mind that it is a process of professional learning, and feedback on lessons is not personal criticism.

Chapter Conclusion

You have had an opportunity to remodel some sample lessons in this chapter, and we trust that you were able to flip through the remainder of the tool kit and see how you might be able to apply the ideas to your own lessons.

We encourage you to use this book in the following ways:

1. Either independently or with a PLC of peers as outlined in Appendix B, use the strategies outlined in this book to remodel existing lessons so that they are infused with creative best practices to better meet the needs of your students.

2. Moving forward, consult the tool kit as you plan your lessons. Begin by identifying your learning expectations or outcomes and devising an assessment plan. Then, flip through the tool kit for ideas to scaffold students' learning up to mastery of the assessment.

We're confident, based on feedback from other teachers who have pilot tested this collection of pedagogies, that you'll find it to be an indispensable resource for remodeling—and eventually planning—your courses, units, and lessons.

3

Present Strategies

Chapter Introduction

This chapter provides you with a series of Present strategies—that is, the strategies introducing students to new material and concepts. Keep in mind that research suggests *that no more than 35% of class-room time should be devoted to the introduction of new material.*

Have your learning outcomes in mind as you view the Present strategies, and make note of those that will best support the subject area and the goals you have established for students. Many of these can be adapted and expanded for use as Apply or Review strategies, and you may make note of those that can be used at different points in your teaching.

Refer to http://www.corwin.com/95strategies to see how each of these strategies aligns with the Common Core State Standards. In addition, note that many of the Present strategies in this chapter have diagnostic assessments built into them, which will allow you to gauge students' prior learning, current knowledge, and comfort with new material during the strategy itself.

STRATEGY 1

Rule or Criteria Induction

Rationale   This strategy builds critical thinking by encouraging students to review examples and develop criteria; they apply inductive reasoning. In addition, it allows students to work cooperatively, contributing to co-construction of knowledge in small groups.

Materials   At least four examples of a class of items (e.g., letters, brochures, an art form, a lab report, equations, etc.)

Description   Students are given examples of the item studied.
In small groups, they review the examples and rank them, best to worst. Next, they identify why they classify some criteria as better or worse. Students record the criteria in small groups.

As a large group, compare the criteria.

Ideal for   Any topic that requires the student to create a work that has to meet particular criteria. Rather than the teacher telling them what is good or bad, students use induction to arrive at criteria. For example, a task such as writing a letter would begin with samples of letters with students applying induction to determine the parts of a letter and criteria for good and bad letter content.

Variation   Provide a placemat to guide their induction (e.g., parts of a letter, effective elements of a composition, ineffective elements, etc.).

STRATEGY 2

Four Corners

| Agree | Strongly Agree | Disagree | Strongly Disagree |

Rationale This strategy allows learners to reflect on an issue or topic as it is introduced and respond accordingly. It also provides a diagnostic assessment for teachers.

By having students pair up with those from an opposing position, students are encouraged to listen to divergent opinions and potentially cultivate critical thinking by considering alterative positions.

Materials Signs posted in each of the four corners of the room reading: Strongly Agree, Agree, Disagree, Strongly Disagree

Description Write a question or statement on the board and have students gather in the corner that best represents their level of agreement. In groups, they can discuss their reasons for that position on the matter.

Group the *strongly agree* and *strongly disagree* groups and the *agree* and *disagree* groups. Ask each individual to find a partner with the opposite position. Partners share their views by listening carefully to the reasons for the opposing position.

At the end of the lesson or unit, repeat this to see if or how students' reactions have changed.

Ideal for Any controversial topic for which students could potentially agree or disagree

Preparation for debate

Four Corners

AGREE

STRONGLY AGREE

DISAGREE

STRONGLY DISAGREE

STRATEGY 3

Snowball

Rationale   This strategy addresses active, kinesthetic learners' needs, while also providing a means of prior learning (or diagnostic) assessment for the teacher.

Materials   Colored paper, each sheet with a multiple-choice question and space for students to place a checkmark. For a class of 30 students, have at least eight snowballs, each with a different question.

Description   Crumple each sheet into a "snowball." Ensure that students have their pens ready, and explain that this is a fast-paced activity. They are to uncrumple the paper, read quickly, place a checkmark next to their response, recrumple, and throw the snowball.

Begin by throwing snowballs out to the class. After a few moments, end the activity by having students throw them back to the teacher.

Ideal for   Gauging prior knowledge or opinion

Cautions   Use colored paper; otherwise, students may crumple their own white paper and confuse the activity.

Not all classes can remain composed during this activity.

When using this activity for the first time, emphasize the need for speed in the reading and passing of snowballs.

STRATEGY 4

The Ladder

Rationale   This strategy offers students visual representation of a particular, complex task, as well as a means of chunking larger tasks into smaller ones. Chunking is consistent with recommendations arising out of brain research for children and adolescents.

Materials   Large (approximately 4 to 5 feet in height) cardboard ladder affixed to a bulletin board or display wall

Sticky notes with student names

Description   Label rungs appropriately for the progression of tasks or knowledge either in a unit of study or for a summative task. Where possible, involve the students in developing content in the rungs in order to encourage learning about breaking larger tasks into smaller ones.

Write the names of students on sticky notes, and move them up the rungs as they progress through subtasks toward a larger summative task.

Ideal for   Any topic or course that requires a progression of tasks or knowledge

Example   Create a Litigation Ladder in preparing for a Mock Trial, with stages of preparation for the trial and hints for each task beneath corresponding rungs.

In a business studies classroom, adapt to a Corporate Ladder. For an entrepreneurial studies class, each rung might represent a section of a venture plan or business plan.

STRATEGY 5

Hot Potato

Rationale   This strategy involves a large group and provides students an opportunity to offer prior knowledge or opinions about a topic, thus contributing to a community of learners. It can also provide diagnostic assessment for the teacher.

Materials   Soft ball, such as a Nerf ball

Questions to start the conversation

Description Have the class stand in a large circle.

Pose the question, and throw the ball to a student to answer it. That student then throws the ball to another student, who then contributes an answer. The process continues until a number of responses are elicited.

Ideal for   Issues that have multiple answers or require students to hold an opinion

A good alternative to brainstorming

Cautions   A raucous class may not be able to handle this activity.

Example   At the beginning of a unit on politics, ask students to name political figures when the potato reaches them.

STRATEGY 6

Graffiti

Rationale   This strategy offers students an opportunity to express them-selves in multiple ways and make sense of new material in a small-group cooperative setting. Students have the opportunity to build on one another's work.

Materials   Markers

Chart paper with a topic or issue in the center to guide discus-sion, one per group

Description   Have students sit in groups, preferably at large tables.

Distribute one graffiti sheet to each group. Students write any-thing they know about the topic, sketch their understanding in graphic form, or pose questions.

After a few minutes (3 to 10, depending on complexity), groups pass their chart paper in a clockwise direction to the next group. Continue this process until all groups have contributed to each sheet of chart paper.

Alternately, the graffiti sheets can remain at single tables, and groups of students can circulate around the room at intervals.

Debrief as a class either by allowing groups to view all com-pleted graffiti sheets or through large-group discussion.

Ideal for   Topics that require opinions or issues that draw on prior knowledge

> ## STRATEGY 7
> *Parking Lot*

Rationale   This strategy allows the reflective learner to respond to a question based on a new issue or new knowledge.

The process of sorting allows students to see others' contributions, while also practicing grouping by criteria, which is conducive to critical thinking development.

Materials   Sticky notes

Parking lot visual—black cardboard with lines marked to represent spots

Description   Pose a question or ask students to contribute their questions about a particular issue. This could be a new topic or a response to a reading.

Students write their responses or questions on sticky notes and contribute them to the parking lot.

As a class, organize the sticky notes into categories and debrief.

Ideal for   Topics that require opinions or issues that draw on prior knowledge

STRATEGY 8

Word Wall

Rationale   This strategy, which is fairly widely used in education, is particularly effective for the visual learner. It allows students to turn to cues to help them identify vocabulary before and during learning and contributes to scaffolding, since new terms and concepts are introduced prior to learning.

Materials   Sticky notes or card stock to record key words

Description   Version 1: Student led

Individually or in groups, students skim a text and identify key words, writing them on sticky notes or card stock.

Version 2: Teacher created

In advance of a new unit, create sticky notes or card stock key words.

Both versions

Tape or pin words to the chalkboard or bulletin board, preferably alphabetically.

Students identify words they know and words that they need help with.

Working in groups, students then help one another with new vocabulary, either explaining words or looking them up together until all students know all vocabulary.

Ideal for   The start of a new unit or chapter

STRATEGY 9

Bingo

B	I	N	G	O
		✪		

Rationale   This strategy allows students to participate in a kinesthetic activity. When bingo cards have carefully considered and relevant questions on them, students can teach one another and share in the construction of knowledge in pairs and small groups.

Materials   Bingo card containing questions or clues relevant to the unit or lesson topic instead of numbers

Prize(s) for first Bingo are optional.

Description   Distribute Bingo cards and allow students a limited period of time to circulate and play. The amount of time required will depend on the complexity of the clues or questions on the bingo card. Structure clues such that students must talk to peers and write down the names of other students (rather than answer independently).

Ideal for   Tacit knowledge or issues

Cautions   Students may not know the rules of Bingo, so be clear when explaining the activity.

Examples   While this can be an effective icebreaker (using clues such as "has a pet," "listens to music," "participates in social networking online," etc.), it can also be used for curricular topics. Other examples include the following:

When teaching forms of business, clues might be "knows a sole proprietor" or "works in a franchise."

When teaching chemistry, each square on the bingo card can represent an element on the periodic table (either number or symbol), and students circulate to fill in all answers from peers.

Bingo

B	I	N	G	O
		★		

STRATEGY 10

Stand Up, Sit Down

Rationale　This large-group activity engages the kinesthetic learner, though it allows all students to engage in some movement, which can be beneficial. Students can share their knowledge or understanding with those who are left with questions. It provides a form of diagnostic assessment for the teacher as well.

Materials　None

Description　Explain that students will stand up if they agree with the statement or sit down if they disagree.

Call out the questions, which can range from "Stand up if you understood the concept from the homework" to curriculum-specific questions. This also provides an opportunity to follow up; allow those who understand to explain to those who do not.

Ideal for　Any topic that requires a yes/no opinion or for diagnostic assessment of the class as a whole

Cautions　None

STRATEGY 11

News Crawl

Rationale	Current events often engage students, help them make connections, and help them see the relevance of a subject or topic to today's world. Brain research suggests that immediate relevancy is important in student learning and retention.
	In addition, this strategy builds on cross-curricular literacy, since it requires students to read a news source and to demonstrate comprehension.
	Various learning styles and preferences are addressed, as students read, record summary points, and orally present.
Materials	Ensure that students have access to news sources.
Description	In advance, assign students dates when they will be responsible for presenting a news item. Provide them with criteria for news items (e.g., must relate to the unit of study or the course/subject as a whole). At the beginning of class, students have 5 minutes to present their news item. Presentations should include the following:
	One- to two-sentence summary of the article
	How the article relates to the course/subject
	Personal reaction to the article
	Three questions that the article raises
	See the News Crawl reproducible for examples.
Ideal for	Virtually any topic that has a current events connection
Cautions	If students are using online news, consider providing a list of reputable sources or provide criteria to evaluate publications, especially for bias and trustworthiness.

REPRODUCIBLE

News Crawl

Name:	Date:
Article title:	
Date published:	
Author:	
Publication or source:	

Brief description:

This is relevant because:

Your reactions and thoughts:

Three questions to generate class discussion based on the news item:

1.

2.

3.

STRATEGY 12

Peer Huddle

Rationale   This strategy promotes cooperative learning in small groups and allows those small groups to co-construct knowledge about a particular issue or question. It also allows for distribution in who participates, since students are called on by assigned number.

Materials   Questions related to curriculum topic

Clock or timer

Description   Students assemble in small groups to form a huddle. Assign a number to each group member (e.g., 1 through 4). The teacher calls out a question, and groups have 30 seconds to discuss and come up with an answer.

When time is up, the teacher calls out a number (e.g., 2) and all 2s stand. The teacher selects one or two 2s to respond to the question on behalf of their group.

Ideal for   Any topic

Cautions   Ensure that students are clear on the format of the activity and their assigned number.

STRATEGY 13

Kid Lit

Rationale   While lower-elementary teachers often use storybooks to introduce a topic, this strategy is not widely used in higher grades. However, anecdotal experience suggests it is highly effective with older learners if the story is relevant and offers a springboard for a discussion about an interesting issue.

Materials   Children's book relevant to the topic for senior grades who may not be accustomed to stories

Blanket for students to sit on when reading (optional)

Description Introduce a topic by reading a children's storybook that touches on key themes. Encourage students to explore the themes and connect storybook content to current events and/or textbook content. Consider having a small class sit on a blanket to create a story-time atmosphere.

Example   To introduce business ethics, environmental issues, waste, and entrepreneurship, use *The Lorax* by Dr. Seuss. To introduce stereotypes, discrimination, and entrepreneurial ethics, use *The Sneetches* by Dr. Seuss. To teach reasoning, critical thinking, and argumentation, use *Don't Let the Pigeon Drive the Bus* by Mo Willems. To introduce concepts such as bias, media, and multiple perspectives, use *The True Story of the Three Little Pigs* by Jon Scieszka.

Ideal for   Virtually any social science or business subject, provided an appropriate book is available. Appropriate storybooks are available for some science topics.

STRATEGY 14

Whip-Around

Rationale   Understanding how others respond to a reading in relation to
one's own response helps to shed light on important themes or
bring to light something an individual missed. This strategy
allows students to hear how their peers reacted to the same
reading and draw conclusions through structured discussion.

Materials   Reading from previous day or week

Description   Students underline one or two lines from a reading that they
responded to most strongly.

Starting at one end of the classroom and moving quickly from
student to student, each student reads the chosen lines aloud,
without commentary.

Once everyone has had a chance to participate, discuss the following as a large group:

- o What lines were repeated?
- o Why do you think that is?
- o What themes or ideas seemed to jump out?

Ideal for   Responses to readings

Cautions   Ensure that all students have completed readings.

STRATEGY 15

Journal Quick Response

Rationale   An individual activity, this strategy guides students' reflections on a reading or video so that they can make sense of what they learned. This strategy is effective for the student who works independently and also contributes to cross-curricular literacy for all.

Materials   Journals for all students

Description   Upon completing a reading or video, have students complete a 3-minute Quick Response in their journals. Suggested guiding questions include these:

What was the main idea of this reading/video?

How does the reading/video connect to our prior learning or knowledge?

What questions does the reading/video raise in your mind?

Ideal for   Responses to readings or videos

Cautions   Ensure that all students have completed readings; students should have experience in journal responses. When introducing this type of response for the first time, model some sample responses and provide criteria for quick response assessment.

STRATEGY 16

Paraphrasing With Synonyms

Rationale   Complicated readings with unfamiliar terminology can over-whelm and disengage students in learning. This strategy helps students systematically break down a complicated reading and work cooperatively to make sense of it.

Materials   None

Description When assigning a reading with new terminology or complex concepts, assign students sections of the reading to paraphrase using synonyms. Once they have done this, students share their sections with peers, indicating the changes so that all students benefit from individual work.

Ideal for   Complex readings

Cautions   Ensure that all students have completed readings.

Provide resources (e.g., dictionary, thesaurus, Internet access) to assist in understanding new terms and arriving at synonyms.

STRATEGY 17

Anagrams

Rationale	Using puzzles can help students focus on new concepts and familiarize themselves with new terminology. This strategy engages students and allows them to learn while participating in a game.
Materials	For teacher-generated version: transparency, slide, or handout with key terms for the lesson in anagram format (letters rearranged to spell other words). A number of online anagram generators can complete these.
	For student-generated version: none
Description	Variation 1: Teacher generated
	Present anagrams to students either projected via LCD or transparency or in the form of a handout.
	Allow students time to come up with answers.
	Variation 2: Student generated
	Allow students time to select key terms from the new unit or lesson and create anagrams for their peers. In small groups, students trade their anagrams and attempt to solve each other's puzzles.
	For both variations: Debrief as a group by allowing students to share answers.
Ideal for	Any topic or reading that includes new vocabulary

STRATEGY 18

What's My Rule?

Rationale   This strategy builds critical thinking by encouraging students to review examples and develop criteria; they apply inductive reasoning.

Materials   One handout per group or students with at least four examples of the application of a rule.

Description   Working individually or in groups, students look at the examples provided and attempt to discern the common rule guiding all of the examples.

Example   In accounting, provide students with a number of balance sheets and ask them to determine rules for balance sheets themselves, as well as how owner's equity is calculated. This can be used for a variety of math and science problems as well.

Ideal for   Any topic or operation that requires a rule to be applied, especially algebra, some sciences, accounting, database management, etc.

STRATEGY 19

Find Your Other Half

Rationale   This strategy allows students to move around while learning, as well as to work with peers to solve the problem of determining matches (and perhaps patterns, depending on the subject area).

Materials   Pairs of concepts, terms, or definitions, with one member of each pair on a separate index card; each student receives one card.

Description   Distribute index cards to students and allow them to circulate in order to find their other half.

Ideal for   Any concepts that contain a number of related pairs

Example   This works well in mathematics, where one half is an operation and the other is the answer.

In addition, this can be used for any subject if the pairs are a term and its definition.

STRATEGY 20

Green-Yellow-Red

Rationale   This strategy allows students to assess their comprehension of new material in a group and teach one another if one student has familiarity and others do not. This strategy also provides a diagnostic assessment of students' comfort with material.

Materials   Three envelopes per group, labeled green, yellow, and red

Index cards with concepts or words from the topic or lesson (one set per group)

Description   In small groups, students go through the index cards one by one and place them in the appropriate envelopes based on the students' collective understanding. The envelopes represent

- o Green: know and can explain
- o Yellow: heard of, but can't explain
- o Red: don't know

Students should assist each other in the small group, sharing their knowledge so that cards in the green envelope are understood by all members in the group.

Debrief as a large group by reviewing all red envelopes and allowing students to explain concepts to peers. Follow with yellow envelopes if necessary.

Ideal for   Any topic that contains specific knowledge or definitions

STRATEGY 21

Human Fold, Pair, and Compare

Rationale   This strategy allows learners to reflect on an issue or topic as it is introduced and respond accordingly; it also addresses kinesthetic learning. Furthermore, it provides a diagnostic assessment for teachers.

Having students pair up with those from an opposing position encourages them to listen to divergent opinions and potentially cultivate critical thinking by considering alternative positions.

Materials   None

Description   Write a question or statement on the board, and have students line up in a single line, based on their level of agreement or disagreement with the issue, such that those who are most in agreement are toward the front, and those in most disagreement are toward the end.

Find the midpoint of the line, and have the line fold in half; this way, those in highest agreement are paired with those in highest disagreement.

Students discuss the issue with the partner standing next to them, with the goal of understanding the reasons for the partner's position on the matter.

Ideal for   Any controversial topic for which students could potentially agree or disagree

Preparation for debate

STRATEGY 22

Clothesline

Rationale	This strategy allows students to share knowledge or opinions by summarizing on a sheet of paper and allows the entire class to learn from the collection of items on the clothesline. It may also be structured to offer diagnostic assessment, depending on the topic or question posed.
	This also provides a visual display that can remain in the classroom for the duration of the unit and be revised if appropriate.
Materials	String or ribbon hung in the classroom at students' eye level
	Clothespins, at least one per student
	Small sheets of paper (ideally in the shape of T-shirts and pants), at least one per student
	Markers
Description	The teacher poses a question or problem to the group.
	Each student writes a response on a small sheet of paper or a cutout of paper clothing (see reproducible) and walks up to the clothesline, affixing it with a clothespin.
	Students should have an opportunity to view their peers' contributions.
	Depending on the topic, students may be encouraged to group responses that share a theme.
Ideal for	Any topic
Example	Prior to performing Internet research, students identify criteria they should consider to determine whether a website is a good source of information on their "clothing." Before starting research, students review all the criteria on the line.

Clothesline T-Shirt

Cut along the T-shirt edges ✂ --

4

Apply Strategies

Chapter Introduction

This chapter provides you with a series of Apply strategies—that is, the strategies encouraging students to actively engage in the new material and concepts introduced in the Present component of the lesson. Keep in mind that research suggests that *at least 60%* of classroom time should be devoted to the application component of the lesson.

Have your learning outcomes in mind as you view the Apply strategies, and make note of those that will best support the subject area and the goals you have established for students. As you make selections, try to vary the approaches to learning over the course of the term or school year to allow students a variety of ways to learn and apply curricular content. While some of the Apply strategies are complex, teachers are encouraged to repeat them from time to time, with the goal that students will be able to master the forms of communication and application within the strategies through ongoing practice.

Refer to http://www.corwin.com/95strategies to see how each of these strategies aligns with the Common Core State Standards.

STRATEGY 23

Three-Member Roles

Rationale   Research tells us that cooperative learning is effective, but it must be structured so that students have clear roles and a sense of purpose in their task. This strategy offers a three-member structure that allows students to play out various roles.

Materials   Interlocking blocks for introduction (optional)

Description   Assign students in groups of three with the roles as shown below. Provide them with an issue to discuss and consider within their roles.

Role:	What you will do:
Observer	Without speaking, carefully watch what the other two members are doing, and take notes. Share your observations at the end of the activity.
Communicator	Do all the talking.
Listener	Talk very little, but you are allowed to ask questions that have yes/no answers.

Begin with an introductory exercise to familiarize students with the concept:

- Provide students with two sets of interlocking blocks.
- The communicator receives one set, the listener the other.
- The communicator and listener sit back-to-back so they cannot see what the other is doing. The observer must sit in a way that he or she can see both.

(Continued)

- The communicator builds a form using the blocks, giving the listener verbal instructions with the intention that the listener will build an identical form.
- The observer watches and takes notes.
- At 3-minute intervals, group members rotate roles until each has played out all three roles.

Once students are acquainted with the roles, assign a problem to which they will apply this cooperative strategy.

Ideal for   Issues that require some level of critical thinking

STRATEGY 24

Socratic Role Play

Rationale   Research tells us that cooperative learning is effective, but it must be structured so that students have clear roles and a sense of purpose in their task. This strategy offers a structure that allows students to play out various roles.

Materials   Paper or chart paper to record notes

Description   In groups of three or more, students respond to a reading or topic in the following roles, rotating their roles every 5 minutes:

- Recorder records questions posed in two columns: those the group answered and those that require further investigation.
- Socrates poses good questions to stimulate peers' thinking about the topic. Socrates can only communicate through questions, not statements.
- Responders are remaining members of the group who respond to Socrates' questions.

Ideal for   Any topic that requires higher-order thinking

Cautions   Model good questions prior to the activity by applying criteria such as these:

- Avoid yes/no answers.
- Focus on higher-order thinking questions—that is, those starting with stems such as *Why, How, What are some reasons for*, etc.

STRATEGY 25

Reading-in-an-Hour

Rationale	Cooperative learning can offer many benefits, including the opportunity for students to work together to complete large tasks within relatively short time frames when work is distributed. This strategy allows a class of students to make sense of a lengthy reading in a short period of time.
Materials	Reading divided into sections that will not exceed 20 minutes of reading time per student or group with assignments for students
	Chart paper and markers
	Clock or timer
Description	Individually or in small groups, students simultaneously read the section assigned to them and make notes to summarize their section in a sentence or two on a sheet of chart paper.
	When reading time is up, in sequence, students present the key points of their sections, thus reconstructing the reading and displaying the chart paper.
Ideal for	Topics that require relatively long readings
Cautions	Preread the material to ensure that it is broken down appropriately and that students can accomplish the task on time.
	Maintain teacher notes so that students' reading notes can be supplemented if necessary.

STRATEGY 26

Social Networking Virtual Role Play

Rationale   Using technology, especially technology that students enjoy, can engage them and encourage them to build literacy skills in untraditional ways. Using social networking for learning offers a highly productive way for students to use their own prior knowledge about technology to live history or literature.

Materials   Computer access to allow students to log in to a social networking site

Description   Identify the key characters in the historical event or literature study and create profiles on a social networking site for them. In advance, create an online group within the social networking site for discussion to take place.

Assign each student a character (for a large class, you may have to create several groups or pair students). Give students the relevant user information so that they can log in.

Students then act out the historical event or plot by updating their status line and communicating with other characters on their walls or in the discussion group. You may also create Memes for them to explore character or historical figure information (e.g., Five Places I've Lived, Ten Random Facts About Me, etc.).

Ideal for   Historical events, novel study, literature study

Example   For example, students could be assigned characters from *The Merchant of Venice* and communicate out the events of the play through status updates on a social networking site.

Cautions   Ensure that students have access to a social networking site.

> ### STRATEGY 27
> *You've Got Mail*

Rationale   Students learn more and are more engaged when they can construct understanding via active engagement and creation. This strategy helps students to build literacy while making sense of course content in the form of correspondence.

Materials   Paper, recycled, or old note cards, postcards, envelopes, etc.

Description Individually or in groups, students create a series of correspondence between two real or historical characters (or invented characters) to demonstrate their understanding of events or arguments.

Ideal for   Historical events, literary plots, or controversial issues

Example   For the controversial issue "Does television have any educational value," students assume the roles of two characters of their own design: the one who agrees with the statement and the other who disagrees. They write three letters to each character, debating the issue, using examples, and citing relevant articles or literature in their letters.

Cautions   Provide students with evaluation criteria ahead of time.

STRATEGY 28

I Read, I Think, Therefore

Rationale   Organizers encourage students to structure their thinking and understanding. This relatively simple organizer encourages students to read and reflect and then draw conclusions.

Materials   I Read, I Think, Therefore organizer, similar to the reproducible on page 68

Description   Assign reading, and distribute the organizer. If the class has not used this format previously, model how it works with a short reading.

Have students complete the organizer with at least three responses.

Ideal for   Response to an assigned reading that requires some interpretation

Variation   Adapt this strategy for video content—I See, I Think, Therefore.

I Read, I Think, Therefore

I read . . .	I think . . .	Therefore . . .

STRATEGY 29

Popcorn Debate

Rationale   Debates are an excellent opportunity for students to cultivate critical thinking and questioning skills since they must take on a position and respond to opposing views. This is a quick version of a debate that involves the entire class. The rapid intervals engage students, and the pace and format allow for creative thinking since each team must think of as many reasons as possible to support its position.

Materials   None

Description   Divide the class into two groups of the same size. Line up the two groups facing one another.

Identify a debate issue, and assign each line a position for or against the issue. Explain that each speaker will have 30 seconds or less to state a reason to support that group's position on the issue.

Each time the teacher says "Pop!" that speaker must conclude, and the floor goes to the corresponding student on the other side of the issue. Speaking opportunities zigzag, and the teacher manages the debate by *popping* at 10- to 30-second intervals, until each student has had the floor at least once.

Ideal for   Any issue or topic with two opposing sides

Caution   Decide in advance if students have the opportunity to pass.

Decide in advance if a score will be kept of responses.

STRATEGY 30

Placemat

Rationale   Research tells us that cooperative learning is effective, but it must be structured so that students have clear roles and a sense of purpose in their task. Working in groups of four or more, students can discuss and structure a response to a question. This strategy also provides diagnostic or prior-learning assessment for teachers.

Materials   Placemat handout, as shown in the reproducible on page 71

Description   Divide students into groups of four or six.

Create placemats with a question in the middle and spaces for each member to respond. Have students individually respond to the question in their space; then discuss as a group.

Debrief as a class by having groups share.

Ideal for   Almost any topic

Six-Person Placemat

SIX-PERSON "PLACEMAT"

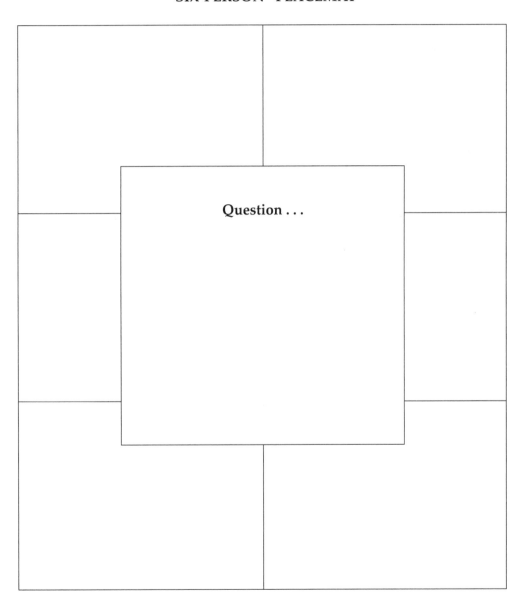

Question . . .

STRATEGY 31

Pizza Parlor

Rationale   This strategy offers a concrete manipulative for students to express an abstract process. Concretizing helps students to understand concepts that may be difficult for them to make sense of otherwise.

Materials   Round cardboard for dough

Colored paper shapes for cheese and various toppings (the number should correspond to the number of steps or components)

Glue and scissors

Description   Explain to students that, in groups, they will create a pizza to represent the task at hand.

Students then assemble the pizza where each topping represents a step in the process. You may encourage them to name their pizzerias.

Students then present their final pizzas to the class, explaining what each topping represents. They may also be required to create a legend.

Display pizzas in the classroom.

Example   In an art history or art appreciation lesson, after viewing examples of art, students would create a pizza in which the toppings represent the elements that go into a good painting. Here is a sample response:

- Double cheese represents technique, since all art starts with good technique, and you need a lot of it.
- Pepperoni represents composition (each slice of pepperoni labeled *line, balance, contrast, proportion, rhythm, unity, texture, color, shape*).
- Anchovies represent the meaning or critique of society, used judiciously, each labeled *status quo, (in)justice, beauty, truth/lies*.
- Green peppers represent medium (each labeled *painting, drawing, sculpture, printmaking, textiles*).

Ideal for   Any topic that requires students to follow sequential steps or put together components; examples include marketing mix, accounting cycle, etc.

STRATEGY 32

Price Is Right

Rationale Games can often be engaging ways to involve students in the curriculum. This variation of a popular television game show allows students to practice their mathematical skills in the context of a large-group competition.

Materials Questions

Chalkboard

Description Assign two students to be a host and a scorekeeper. Allow students to play in teams so that everyone is involved. You may wish to establish three teams and have one representative of each team participating at the board simultaneously while team members watch.

Pose questions to the group that require a ranking or mathematical answer. The representatives at the board respond, with the team closest to the correct number without going over winning each round.

Ideal for Any lesson that requires mathematics or ranking, such as retail pricing, tax spending, financial statement analysis, financial budgeting, etc.

Cautions Plan questions in advance and have more questions ready than you think you need.

Not all students will be familiar with the rules of this game, so be clear in advance.

STRATEGY 33

Thinking Hats

Rationale Combined with the idea of parallel thinking, which is associated with it, this strategy provides a means for groups to think together more effectively and a means to plan thinking processes in a detailed and cohesive way.

Materials Groupings and role assignments

Case study or issue for discussion

Description Distribute the case or issue; students play out the roles listed below to come to a conclusion.

Hat	Meaning	Tasks
White Hat	Calls for information known or needed	This person keeps asking questions about what's missing. What don't we know? What do we need to find out?
Red Hat	Signifies feelings, hunches, and intuition	This person uses his or her instincts and responds from the gut and from emotion.
Yellow Hat	Symbolizes values and benefits and uncovers why something may work	This person looks at the morality of the problem in connection with society and looks out for the best interests of all.
Black Hat	Is judgment—the devil's advocate or why something may not work	This person looks for the downfall in the argument and questions all ideas and thoughts.

Green Hat	Focuses on creativity— possibilities, alternatives, and new ideas	This person says "what if" and tries to get others to see new ways of thinking or visualizing.
Blue Hat	Used to manage the thinking process	This person organizes the data and connects all the ideas together by summarizing.

Ideal for   Issues or case studies with no right answer for which teams have to come to a solution

Cautions   Playing the roles effectively may take practice, so be sure to repeat this strategy.

| STRATEGY 34 |

Debate

Rationale   Debates engage students in their learning by forcing them to deal with complexity while providing relevancy of course material to everyday issues and also cultivating collaboration and oral communication skills.

Materials   Instructions, details about issue to debate

Description   Individually or in groups, students construct an argument for a debate. Provide the following instructions:

- In one sentence, describe the issue you are debating. What is your position on the issue for the purpose of the debate (are you for it or against it)?
- Give three reasons for your position.
- Give at least two facts to back up each reason you have.
- Sum up the reasons in one concluding sentence.
- Make a list of all the possible things opponents might say to argue the other position.
- For each opposing argument, come up with a response (rebuttal) that supports your case. Use facts whenever possible.

Have students map out their debates using a rough guideline such as the one below. Encourage scripts.

1st minute   Define your speech. Explain the point you will be trying to make and how you will make it. State your argument in a single, short sentence. Define your team's strategy, explaining what others in your group will say (or have said).

2nd minute   Lay out your argument. It is best to propose or oppose on three points (e.g., political, economic, social, etc.). This means you should have three reasons for your argument. In a sentence, let the audience know what the three points of your argument will be.

3rd to 5th minute	Address each part of your argument that you laid out in the 2nd minute. Provide details about each.
6th minute	Sum up your argument in a concluding sentence.
Ideal for	Issues that have no clear right or wrong answers
Cautions	Students will need ample time to prepare.
	Since debates require structure, guidance is necessary to help them chunk their tasks.

REPRODUCIBLE

Debate Organization Sheet

1. Construct an Argument for a Debate

In one sentence, describe the **issue** you are debating.	
What is your **position** on the issue for the purpose of the debate (are you for it or against it)?	
Give **three reasons** for your position.	
Give at least **two facts** to back up each reason you have.	
Sum up the reasons in **one concluding** sentence.	
Make a list of all the possible things your **opponents** might say to argue the other position.	
For each of the opposing arguments, come up with a response (**rebuttal**) that supports your case. Use facts whenever possible.	

2. Map Out Your Debate

The following is a rough guideline to help you structure your speech. Write out a script and remember to prepare your rebuttal in addition to the speech shown below.

1st minute	Define your speech. Explain the point you will be trying to make and how you will make it. State your argument in a single, short sentence. Define your team's strategy explaining what others in your group will say (or have said).
2nd minute	Lay out your argument. It is best to propose or oppose on three points (e.g., political, economic, social, etc.). This means you should have three reasons for your argument. In a sentence, let the audience know what the three points of your argument will be.
3rd to 5th minute	Address each part of your argument that you laid out in the 2nd minute. Provide details about each.
6th minute	Sum up your argument in a concluding sentence.

REPRODUCIBLE

Debate Organizer

Name: _____ Date: _____

Topic: _____

My debate position on the topic: _____

Introduction

_____

_____

_____

_____

_____

Reasons and facts (remember to cite your sources!)

_____

_____

_____

_____

_____

Conclusion

_____

_____

_____

_____

_____

(Continued)

(Continued)

Possible objections from your opponent(s)

_____

_____

_____

_____

_____

Other notes

_____

_____

_____

_____

_____

Debate Peer Evaluation

Evaluated by: _____

Name of group evaluated: _____ Date: _____

While observing the debate, evaluate the performance. Circle the most appropriate grade where *1* indicates that the group needs additional work, and *5* indicates that the group is outstanding.

Clear opening statement in which the position was stated	① ② ③ ④ ⑤
Three good reasons to support their position	① ② ③ ④ ⑤
Three reasons backed up with two facts for each	① ② ③ ④ ⑤
Brief conclusion that summed up their argument	① ② ③ ④ ⑤
Appropriate and effective speaking style (e.g., language, eye contact, tone, volume, etc.)	① ② ③ ④ ⑤
Appropriate body language (e.g., gestures, movement, walking around)	① ② ③ ④ ⑤
Response to their opponent with well-planned arguments	① ② ③ ④ ⑤
Thorough knowledge of the subject	① ② ③ ④ ⑤
Appeared organized and prepared for the debate	① ② ③ ④ ⑤
Mark (add up all the numbers you circled)	/45

STRATEGY 35

Mock Trial

Rationale   Like debates, mock trials engage students in their learning by forcing them to deal with complexity while also providing relevancy of course material to everyday issues; they also cultivate collaboration and oral communication skills.

Materials   Any relevant text as a basis for the case (see examples)

An organizer for the mock trial agenda (see description)

Classroom set up for trial

Gavel, costumes (optional)

Description   Involve students in an exploration of how trials operate, arriving at an agenda, such as the following:

- Judge (teacher) presents the case and advises the jury (2 minutes)
- Prosecution opening statement (2 minutes)
- Defense opening statement (2 minutes)
- Prosecution direct examination (5 minutes)
- Defense cross-examination (5 minutes)
- Defense direct examination (5 minutes)
- Prosecution cross-examination (5 minutes)
- Prosecution closing (2 minutes)
- Defense closing (2 minutes)
- Judge advisement (2 minutes)

Assign roles to students and design roles based on case; witnesses, defendant, and complainant should be from the text or historical event, whereas roles such as prosecutor and jurors are at the teacher's discretion. Define success criteria for all roles.

Either construct with students or provide a work plan for their tasks.

Allow ample time for students to prepare for their roles through research and scripting (approximately two 60-minute periods).

As a class, perform the mock trial (approximately 40 minutes).

Ideal for   Complex issues that have multiple solutions or positions and have a legal connection, whether from the news, history, or literature

Examples   While many issues for mock trials are apparent in the news, this strategy works well to investigate historical or literary events. For instance, stories such as "The Three Little Pigs" and "Little Red Riding Hood" can be explored as mock trials (e.g., the Big Bad Wolf is suing Red Riding Hood for defamation of character).

Cautions   Mock trials require preparation on the part of students, so allow ample time for preparation.

If additional research is necessary, consider offering students a range of preselected resources to focus their investigation.

Since mock trials are somewhat complex and require a variety of subtasks, consider using an organizer (such as a Litigation Ladder described in Strategy 4 on page 37) to help students organize their time and tasks.

STRATEGY 36

Think-Pair-Share

Rationale   This strategy gives students an opportunity to process information, formulate ideas (develop thinking), and then share
thoughts with others (communication). It allows all students to
actively participate in learning when time or class size does not
permit full class participation.

Materials   Questions or issues for students to contemplate

Description   Students are given individual think time to respond to a question, problem, or new information. After a short period of think
time, students are asked to find a partner, pair up, and share the
information. Once the pairs reach consensus, they are asked to
share their information with the class.

Ideal for   Topics that require opinions

Cautions   Limit the time to ensure that students stay on track.

> **STRATEGY 37**
>
> *Think-Pair-Square*

Rationale   Like Think-Pair-Share, this strategy gives students an opportunity to process information, formulate ideas (develop thinking), and then share thoughts with others (communication). It allows all students to actively participate in learning when time or class size does not permit full class participation. It allows for discussion in larger groups than Think-Pair-Share, so that students can help one another and learn from each other's opinions, knowledge, or reactions.

Materials   Questions or issues for students to contemplate

Description   This is a variation of Think-Pair-Share (previous strategy). Combine two pairs for an added level of conversation, thus creating a *square*. In the square, pairs share their responses with another pair instead of with the whole class.

Ideal for   Topics that require opinions

Cautions   Limit the time to ensure students stay on track.

STRATEGY 38

Jigsaw-Expert Group

Rationale   This strategy has been associated with long-term learning effectiveness when the group engages in problem solving (Michaelsen, Fink, & Knight, 1997).

It allows students to actively participate in learning (rather than passively receiving information) and allows for greater interaction.

Materials   None

Description   Variation 1: Homogeneous home groups

Groups are established, each group is assigned a topic, and each team member is responsible for learning about that topic. Thus, each group is an expert on one topic.

Each expert meets with members of other groups who are expert in other topics—this reshuffling of the groups is the jigsaw component. After sharing information in the newly formed groups, each expert returns to his or her own group.

Variation 2: Diverse groups

Students start in a home team of three to four, and each student on the team is given a different reading or topic to learn, with the intent that *each* group member will be an expert on something different. Once students have a chance to establish their expertise, they teach what they have learned to other members of the group.

Ideal for   Sets of interrelated topics or when there are multiple readings for a topic

Example   Examples include

- The four *P*'s of marketing where groups represent product, price, place, and promotion
- A history lesson that includes multiple perspectives on a particular event

Cautions   Have groups established ahead of time, with clear directions to ensure that they understand their topic and what to do once groups are "jigsawed."

STRATEGY 39

What If?

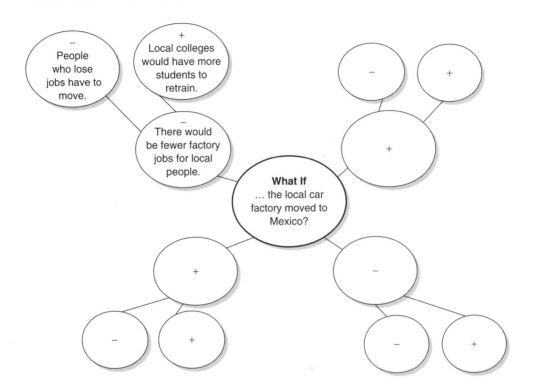

Rationale   This strategy allows students to think laterally and engages the visual learner in particular.

It can be completed individually or in groups.

Materials   What If graphic organizer format, as shown in the above figure. This might be reproduced for students, or students could view an example and create their own.

Description   Individually or in groups, students complete the graphic organizer based on a problem or question provided by the teacher.

Ideal for   Topics that lead to a variety of outcomes

Cautions   Be very specific in your problem or question.

What If?

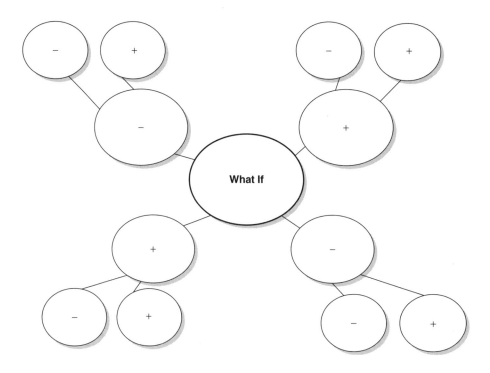

STRATEGY 40

Reaction Wheel

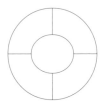

Rationale   This strategy allows students to think laterally and engages the visual learner while drawing on peers to cooperate in reacting to ideas. As a group, students can compare reactions and learn from one another while thinking critically in order to identify areas of agreement in the center of the organizer.

Materials   Chart paper and markers for groups to create their organizers

Description Working in groups of four, students complete the reaction wheel in response to a reading, presentation, or concept. First, groups discuss the topic. They record common reactions or things they agree on in the center. Then, each team member records unique perspectives or areas of disagreement in each of the four outer quadrants, as per the reproducible on page 90.

Ideal for   Any topic

Reaction Wheel

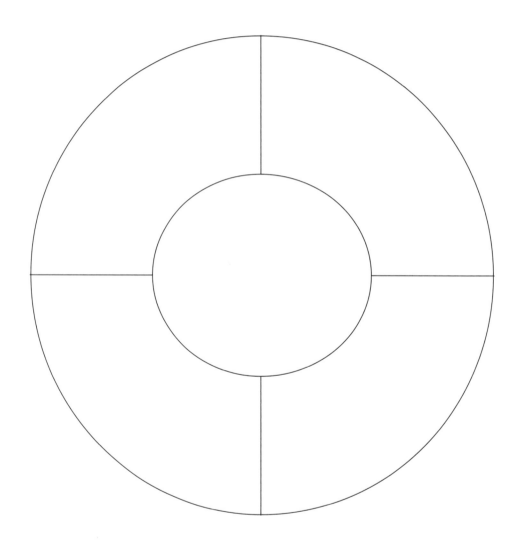

STRATEGY 41

Peanut Butter Sandwich

Rationale   This strategy requires students to focus on clarity of communication, thus building their oral communication skills.

Materials   Bag containing two or more slices of bread, peanut butter, spreading knife, or spoon

Description Students are told to pretend that the teacher is an alien from another planet, and they are to give instruction on how to make a peanut butter sandwich. The teacher receives the verbal instructions from the students but takes the instructions literally, thus making mistakes. For example, if a student begins by saying, "Put peanut butter on the bread," the teacher would place the jar of peanut butter on the bread. In this activity, students develop awareness of clear communication.

Students then apply their learning to a concrete task related to the subject area.

Ideal for   Introduction of a unit or section that requires attention to good communication (e.g., computer programming, accounting, mathematical operations, etc.)

Cautions   Teacher should demonstrate; students might make assumptions and fail to illustrate the task.

STRATEGY 42

Brick

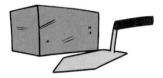

Rationale   Analyzing a situation or a phenomenon through multiple lenses is an important critical thinking skill. This strategy requires students to identify different perspectives and to analyze a text, situation, or concept through each of those lenses. It also allows for alternate ways of self-expression since the Brick enables creative representation of ideas.

Materials   Boxes (e.g., tissue box), glue, scissors, magazines, and pictures for cutouts

Description Students are given a topic, issue, or case study to work with. Individually or in groups, they explore various perspectives on the topic and represent their thoughts on different sides of the brick by labeling, decorating, and explaining what each side represents.

Ideal for   Either a topic with multiple lenses for understanding (e.g., law, ethics, etc.) or a topic with many facets

Example   A human rights injustice could be examined from a legal lens, an ethical lens, a cultural lens, and a gender lens. Each of these lenses would be reflected on a separate side of the brick through words, phrases, or images.

Brick

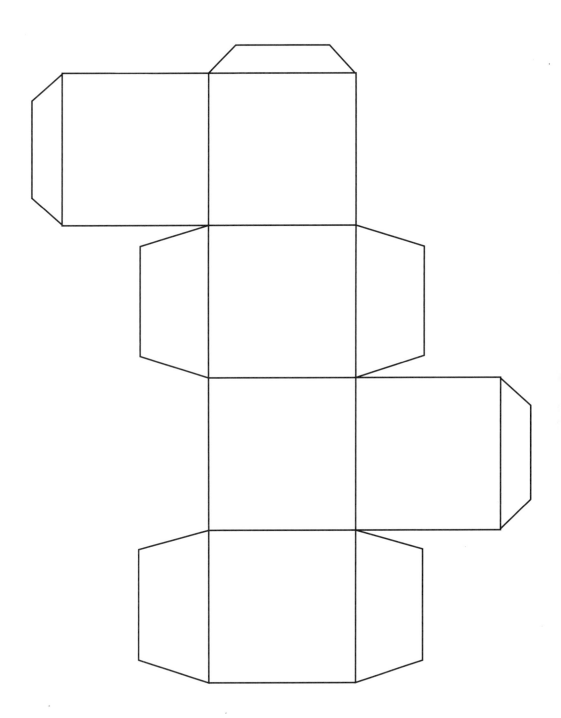

STRATEGY 43

Diamond Ranking

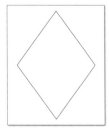

Rationale   Analyzing a reading or a video in order to discern most important and less important information is an important skill; however, it takes practice. This strategy offers students a visual organizer to help them work through content in a structured way. If they use this strategy in a group setting, students can discuss and come to a consensus about the relative importance of information.

Materials   Chart paper or paper, pens

Description   In response to a reading, presentation, or video, students working in small groups use a diamond-shaped configuration to organize the main points.

The most important point goes at the top of the diamond, two statements of lesser but equal importance go below, and statements of moderate importance go beneath both of those. Finally, the statement of least importance goes at the bottom of the diamond.

Ideal for   Any reading, presentation, or video

Cautions   Model the structure for students in advance so that they understand how to apply the visual organizer.

REPRODUCIBLE

Diamond

STRATEGY 44

Five W's

Rationale   Deconstructing a reading or video to identify its components is an important literacy-building process. This strategy provides students with organizers through which they can practice identifying the components of a reading or video.

Materials   Handout containing a table to organize the five *W*'s

Description   In response to a reading, students identify the five *W*'s:

- Who
- What
- Where
- When
- Why

Ideal for   Case study or news formats

REPRODUCIBLE

Five W's

Topic: _____ Name: _____	
Who?	
What?	
Where?	
When?	
Why?	

STRATEGY 45

Dear Abby

Rationale   This strategy builds cross-curricular literacy, since students compose questions. In addition, it builds students' ability to pose good questions and allows them to actively engage in learning with peers.

Materials   Index cards

Description   In small groups, students compose a Dear Abby question for their peers in response to the topic, a reading, or other lesson content.

Once each group has composed a letter to Abby, groups pass their cards in a clockwise fashion. On the first pass, groups compose a response on a separate sheet of paper. On the subsequent passes, groups edit previous responses until each group receives its original letter back.

As an alternative variation, the teacher can compose the letters for students' response.

Ideal for   Topics that require students to create solutions to problems; this may be historical figures faced with problems, literary figures faced with problems in a novel or play, or situations such as ethical or legal issues.

STRATEGY 46

Who or What Am I?

Rationale	This strategy allows students to work cooperatively, contributing to co-construction of knowledge while also challenging them to engage in questioning and inductive reasoning.
Materials	Stickers or labels with concepts, characters, or historical figures related to the unit of study
Description	Circulate around the room and place a sticker on each student's back, ensuring that students refrain from telling their peers what the stickers say.
	Students have 5 minutes to circulate while asking yes/no questions to determine what concept, figure, or character is on their backs.
Ideal for	Almost any topic
Cautions	Give clear directions and demonstrate some sample questions (e.g., Am I a person? Am I a formula? Can I be used to solve an equation?) before placing stickers on students' backs.

> **STRATEGY 47**
>
> *Five E's*

Rationale   Deconstructing a reading or video to identify its components is an important literacy-building process. This strategy provides students with organizers through which they can practice identifying the components of a reading or video.

Materials   Access to a computer lab or library for the Explore component

Description   Follow the Five *E's* to structure this exploration:

Engage: Define the topic for investigation by connecting it to students' experience or interest.

Explore: Small groups of students who will work collaboratively on the task identify a question that they wish to explore related to the topic. Groups research their question.

Explain: Groups share their findings with the class by answering the question in a defined period of time (e.g., 10 minutes).

Elaborate: Groups involve the class in their explanation by inviting the class to expand on concepts, provide examples, or connect their presentation to other information.

Evaluate: Individuals provide a self-evaluation of their process in writing.

Ideal for   Any topic, but adjust time allotted for Five *E's* to the complexity of the topic.

Cautions   Groups should be carefully selected, and criteria for presentations and evaluations must be provided in advance.

STRATEGY 48

Wired Knowledge

Rationale   This strategy allows students to apply learning visually and kinetically, and it also involves the use of concrete manipulatives to express abstractions.

Materials   One two- to three-foot piece of light, bendable wire or pipe cleaner per group

Description   In small groups, students use the wire to construct a visual illustration of a phenomenon, which could include trends, patterns, events, fluctuations, etc.

Students should make notes of what the bends and angles in the wire represent.

Groups present their wires to the class, comparing and noting similarities and differences.

Ideal for   Tasks that have a timeline (e.g., plot of a literary work, historical timeline, etc.) or graphic representation (e.g., economic cycles, product life cycle, etc.)

Cautions   Ensure that students use the wire or pipe cleaner safely.

STRATEGY 49

Milling to Music

Rationale   This strategy taps into musical intelligence; it also allows students to move around and expend physical energy. It builds oral communication skills and allows for consideration of a topic or theme at the same time.

Materials   Radio or computer with speakers and music ready to be played

Watch or timer

Description   While the music is playing, students mill around the room. When the music stops, let them have 60 seconds to discuss a structured question with the person closest to them.

Once 60 seconds is up, restart the music, and repeat the process until all structured questions designed by the teacher are complete.

Ideal for   Higher-order thinking topics that require discussion or exchange of ideas

Cautions   Walk around while discussions are taking place to ensure that students are on task.

Have ample questions in advance of the activity to ensure smooth transitions. Consider having the questions ready on chart paper or transparencies to avoid writing or repeating.

STRATEGY 50

Scrapbook

Rationale	Current events often engage students, help them make connections, and show them the relevance of a subject or topic to today's world. Brain research suggests that immediate relevancy is important in student learning and retention. Because this activity requires students to collect information from news/magazine sources, it taps into that form of engagement.
	In addition, this strategy builds on inductive reasoning, since it requires students to look for themes among clippings.
Materials	Either access to the Internet or access to newspapers, magazines, or other readings relevant to the topic.
Description	Students collect materials over a set period of time (e.g., week, month, term, or semester) on a particular topic. Once they have collected the information, students create a summary of their collection and identify key trends.
	This strategy can also be adapted for online research since students can collect links on a wiki, blog, or specific linking website.
Example	Students explore careers in science over the course of one semester, adding jobs advertisements on a weekly basis to their scrapbook. At the end of the semester, students summarize types of jobs and skills/knowledge required for a career in science.
Ideal for	Topics that require ongoing investigation or information from a variety of sources such as current events, career exploration, etc.

STRATEGY 51

Reason to Roam

Rationale   This strategy taps into musical intelligence; it also allows students to move around and expend physical energy. It builds oral communication skills and allows for consideration of a topic or theme at the same time.

Materials   Handout in which the page provides space for each topic to be summarized

Clock or timer

Description   Assign a topic to groups of four students. Each group is responsible for either researching or reading up on the assigned topic, making them experts.

Within each group, two students take the role of *roamers*, and two stay put. With handouts and pens, roamers move from group to group at 5-minute intervals and write down information as they converse with other groups.

Once all roaming is done, roamers return and share information with the remaining members of their group.

Ideal for   Any topic for which expert topics can be assigned

Cautions   Teachers must be very specific to ensure that students remain on task and that discussions remain focused.

STRATEGY 52

Trading Cards

Rationale   Students learn more and are more engaged when they can construct understanding via active engagement and creation. This strategy helps students to build literacy while making sense of course content in the form of trading cards.

Moreover, sets of trading cards can be used to teach younger grades as a follow-up activity.

Materials   Either access to a computer lab, if cards will be created electronically, or cardboard, glue, paper, magazines, etc.

Sign-up sheet for students to claim their topics

Description   Either alone or in groups, students create trading cards to represent key information from a unit of study. Students or groups may each be assigned a different topic to allow for a range of different cards.

Ideal for   A multitude of topics or subjects

Examples   Trading cards could be created for

- Periodic table of elements
- Types of businesses
- Pieces of legislation
- Historical or literary figures
- Historical dates
- Geographic locations
- Weather patterns

STRATEGY 53

Shrinking Your World

Rationale   This strategy allows students to apply concepts in a concrete way by mapping particular items, processes, or events. They can make sense of how a particular practice applies to their own lives or a larger community.

Materials   Provide each student with several sticky notes and a map of your community (neighborhood, city, or town) printed from an online mapping service or a world map, depending on the topic.

Description   Clearly define the situation they are to map.

If research is necessary, allow students ample time to gather data.

Provide time for students, individually, in a small group, or in a large group, to map their research.

Ideal for   Any topic that has a geographic element

Examples   Mapping can be adapted to all sorts of topics:

- Local impacts of practices, such as recycling paths in the local community
- Supply chain management, such as mapping all the locations for materials and production for a commonly used product (e.g., a shirt, a bottle of soda, etc.)
- Identifying what parts of the world a reading refers to
- Mapping historical events

STRATEGY 54

Text-to-Self

Rationale   Making personal connections with a reading helps students to internalize and comprehend it. This strategy provides structure for students to consider their own personal connection to a reading.

Materials   None

Description   This strategy requires students to reflect on material with a focus on how it relates to them. Upon reading or viewing, students record their answers to these questions:

- How does this remind me of my life and experiences? How is it different?
- What prior knowledge do I have that might connect to this? What books, stories, poems, songs, or movies or other media does this remind me of? Why?

Ideal for   Most readings, videos

STRATEGY 55

Venn Diagrams

Rationale   This strategy allows students to engage in visual learning and make connections between and across ideas. This assists with lateral thinking.

Materials   None necessary, though Venn diagrams can be done on a large scale as classroom displays or electronically.

Description   Individually or in groups, students create a Venn diagram to represent related concepts. Students label the circles appropriately to show elements of overlap and uniqueness.

Ideal for   Related concepts within a unit of study, a topic, or a literary work

STRATEGY 56

Reflection Wall

Rationale   Students benefit from the ability to make personal connections and see others' reflections, thus applying abstract concepts to concrete examples. The second step of this strategy allows students to sort examples, which builds inductive reasoning.

Materials   Distribute index cards or sticky notes to all students.

Description   In response to a reading or video, students anonymously record their reaction. The response can be a word, a sentence, or a paragraph. Next, students stick their responses to a board or wall.

As a second step, the class may categorize their responses (e.g., positive, negative, neutral), rearranging them as they go. Alternately, the class can identify themes for categorization.

Ideal for   Any topic that generates a student reaction or opinion

STRATEGY 57

Case Study Roles

Rationale   Case studies allow students to apply abstract concepts or rules to real life or simulated situations. However, without structured guidance on solving a case study, groups may not perform well. This strategy offers roles to be assigned to students so that each member is working constructively.

Materials   Case studies, one per group

Description   Assign the following organizational roles:

- Synthesizer (summarizes information)
- Recorder (takes notes)
- Presenter (shares information with the class)
- Timekeeper (ensures that all are on task and allots time for questions at the end of the case study)

All team members participate in finding solutions to the case study, but they also adhere to their assigned organizational roles.

Ideal for   Case studies for any subject area

Cautions   Model how to approach a solution, or provide criteria for an appropriate solution for your subject area.

STRATEGY 58

Create a Puzzle

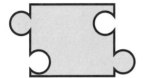

Rationale	This strategy allows students to think about connections between and among concepts in a particular topic or theme. They express the connections visually in the form of a puzzle. This also allows the active learner to create a concrete representation of an abstract topic.
Materials	Paper, scissors, markers
Description	Individually or in groups, students create a jigsaw puzzle to show interconnected parts of a concept learned.
	Students should exchange puzzles and attempt to complete one another's, providing formative feedback to the puzzle designer(s).
Ideal for	Curriculum that has interrelated concepts and topics

STRATEGY 59

Fishbowl

Rationale   This strategy allows students to participate in making sense of a concept or problem in several ways—some students discuss (demonstrating oral communication) while others record (demonstrating written communication).

Materials   None

Description   A small group of students discusses a controversial topic in front of the class. Students not participating in the presentation take notes as they listen and write a quick position paper at the end of class.

                  If possible, allow several groups to discuss during the lesson to ensure that all students have the opportunity to both speak and write.

Ideal for   Any topic that contains a controversial issue

STRATEGY 60

Talking Chips

Rationale   The rapid intervals of this strategy engage students, and the pace and format allow for creative thinking since each individual quickly comes up with a response. This also allows for full-class participation since the limited number of chips students receive ensures that all students have an opportunity to contribute.

Materials   Inexpensive poker chips or other similar manipulatives at a ratio of three chips per student

Description   Use chips to mediate student discussion and ensure that all students have an opportunity to participate. If using various colored chips, assign types of contributions (e.g., blue is a question, red is a statement, etc.).

As students respond, collect the chips and make formative notes on individual participation.

Ideal for   Topics that generate discussion; it is useful for classes where some students have a tendency to dominate conversation.

Cautions   Determine in advance if you will allow students to give their chips to a peer.

STRATEGY 61

Show-Do, Do-Show

Rationale   Some tasks require modeling, and this strategy allows for a slightly more interactive approach than purely passive learning by students. Following the pattern of show-do, do-show, students participate within a defined and structured rhythm of active and passive.

Materials   Vary depending on the topic

Description In a variation on pure demonstration, the teacher first models a task with students following along. Next, student volunteers model a similar task (or variant on a task), and their peers and the teacher observe and give feedback.

Ideal for   Any topic that requires students to follow a procedure (e.g., computing, math, some sciences)

STRATEGY 62

Round Robin or Round Table

Rationale   The rapid intervals of this strategy engage students, and the pace and format allow for creative thinking since each individual quickly comes up with a response. This also allows for full-class participation.

Materials   Paper and pens

Description   First, the teacher poses a question. In groups, students circulate a piece of paper and a pen. A student writes one response and then says it out loud. The student passes the paper and pen to the left, and the process is repeated for 5 to 10 minutes. Students may pass their turn at any time. Once time is called, students discuss their answers or solutions with another group or with the entire class.

Ideal for   The key to this strategy is the question or the problem students are discussing; it must have the potential for a number of different right answers.

> **STRATEGY 63**
>
> *Carousel Seminars*

Rationale   This strategy allows groups to engage in problem solving and peer teaching. It lets students actively participate in learning (rather than passively receiving information) and allows for greater interaction.

Materials   None—students create their own materials

Description   In groups of five, students create rotating miniseminars for the class. Student roles are as follows:

- One student is responsible for a large-group introduction to the topic (10 minutes).
- Three students are responsible for *each* creating concurrent rotating activities on three separate subtopics (10 minutes each). During the concurrent sessions, the class is divided into thirds and rotates through small groups.
- One student is responsible for timing, summarizing, and final remarks for the large group (5 minutes).

Ideal for   Topics that allow for student-driven seminars with senior grades

Cautions   Model the process once before class assignments; provide students with evaluation criteria in advance.

Ter This strategy can be used with any age-group, though younger students require more structure and guidance.

Consider previewing students' plans in advance of seminars to offer feedback if they miss key points or require further advice.

STRATEGY 64

Scavenger Hunt

Rationale   This strategy allows groups to engage in problem solving by active investigation. Students actively participate in learning (rather than passively receiving information) and can interact.

This strategy can be done as an online activity or a physical scavenger hunt in the school.

It can be applied to virtually any topic and is effective at all age and grade levels if the level of challenge is appropriate for students.

Materials   If online:

- In advance, identify websites that students should visit for information. Be sure that the questions are designed so that students have to read the websites to respond correctly.

If in school:

- Gather ample materials for all groups to obtain.
- Ensure that you have permission if using school space outside your classroom.

Description   Using a guide (see the reproducible on page 119), students actively seek out information or items to guide their learning. For example:

- Distribute the guide and ensure that all students understand what is expected (15 minutes).
- Divide students into groups and provide ample time for them to explore and locate information or items (30 minutes to several hours, depending on the task).
- Provide time to debrief so that students can share their responses (15 minutes or more, depending on the topic).

(Continued)

(Continued)

Ideal for   Online scavenger hunts are ideal for just about any topic since students can explore all subject areas online.

Physical scavenger hunts are particularly good for the natural sciences, as students can locate flora and fauna on the school grounds and report back.

Cautions   • In a physical scavenger hunt, ensure that there are ample clues for all groups or students to locate.
• Carefully monitor progress, as groups may not complete the hunt simultaneously. If a group or an individual is falling behind, step in with additional clues to assist.

Variations   Consider using an online WebQuest template to structure the investigation.

Consider offering different objectives to different groups and combining this with a jigsaw/expert group technique for debrief.

REPRODUCIBLE

Scavenger Hunt Guide

Name: _____ Date: _____

Scavenger Hunt theme: _____

Objective 1: _____	
Clues:	
Places to visit:	
Question 1:	
Question 2:	
Question 3:	

Objective 2: _____	
Clues:	
Places to visit:	
Question 4:	
Question 5:	
Question 6:	

(Continued)

(Continued)

Objective 3: _____

Clues:

Places to visit:

Question 7:	
Question 8:	
Question 9:	

STRATEGY 65

Passport Stations

Rationale   This strategy allows groups to engage in problem solving by active investigation. It lets students actively participate in learning (rather than passively receiving information) and allows for greater interaction.

Materials   Passports with pages for each station can be created in a desktop publishing program in the form of booklets. You may have questions to answer, or even a rubric, for stations to track their participation.

Stamps for each station to indicate successful completion

Materials for each station

Description Set up four or five stations at which students can explore a different theme as they circulate through the stations. Ensure that each station will take approximately the same amount of time to complete. The sorts of activities that can occur at stations include the following:

- A brief reading for senior grades
- A sorting activity
- An examination of examples to identity criteria
- A reflection-type activity
- A graffiti-type activity in which groups build on earlier visitors' work on chart paper
- Puzzle
- Small experiment

Group students and have them circulate through stations at timed intervals. The teacher must circulate and ensure that all are on task and no difficulties arise.

Ideal for   Any subject or topics

(Continued)

(Continued)

Cautions　　Passport stations require careful planning on the part of the teacher in order to establish self-contained activity that adheres to the timing. However, even in the senior grades, students enjoy the variety and fast pace that well-planned passport stations offer.

Examples　　• In the elementary grades, stations can be cross-curricular, representing different subjects along a theme. A mystery theme might include a reading, a game, a series of clues to put together, and so forth.
　　　　　　　　• In the senior grades, stations are typically within a subject area but explore different themes. Science passport stations might include methods, materials, and small experiments. Marketing stations might include an exploration of each of the four *P*'s as independent stations, with examples of items for which students must examine the things at the station and draw conclusions about the marketing mix at that station.

STRATEGY 66

Café Conversations

Rationale   Students can learn from vibrant discussion with their peers. Setting up a café-style debate in which students assume roles or characters allows for valuable perspective taking and seeing an issue from many sides.

Materials   None required, but the desks should be arranged café style if possible with small tables for discussion.

Description   Before using the strategy, consider if you wish students to discuss a topic in a general sense, or if you wish to assign the roles, characters, or perspectives. This will depend on the topic to be discussed.

In groups of three to four, students gather at café tables and discuss the issue at hand, either playing roles or perspectives or from their own understandings. Allow at least 30 minutes for discussion.

Consider a follow-up, large-group debrief.

Ideal for   Any topic that requires thought or reflection, especially one with controversial issues

Cautions   If students lack practice in small group discussion, consider generating a class list of norms and expectations for civil discussion.

Examples   Examples include the following:

- In teaching any second language, café conversations can be unstructured but adhering to a topic to practice the language.
- In studying ethical dilemmas, assign students to utilitarian and deontological roles.
- In studying a legal issue, students can take opposing perspectives on a particular case or dilemma.
- In studying history, students can take on the roles of major historical figures and role-play a relevant topic to that historical period.

STRATEGY 67

Virtual Museum

Rationale   Virtual Museum is a collaborative digital space that includes student-produced oral, visual, and written items for a particular theme.

This strategy allows groups to engage in problem solving by active investigation and create an exhibit for a class museum. It allows students to actively participate in learning (rather than passively receiving information) and allows for greater interaction. The use of technology will engage many students, and they ultimately learn from each other's work rather than textbooks or third-party sources.

Finally, the flexibility in ways to create exhibits for the museum ought to allow for multiple intelligences to be addressed.

Materials   Library and/or lab time for research

A variety of media to create exhibits for the virtual museum such as presentation software, digital cameras, webcams, and scanners

A digital platform to house the exhibits; this could be online space in the form of a website or wiki, or it can be housed on a DVD, ideally created using software (such as web authoring software) to allow users to click on themes and topics to progress through the material.

Description • Decide what format the virtual museum will take (website, wiki, DVD, or other) and ensure that you have access to the technology and resources to finalize the museum.
               • In advance, decide if students will work independently or in groups for an exhibit. Most likely, this decision will be dependent on the number of topics available within the theme.

- Assign an exhibit topic within a theme to students and clarify the scope of their research, as well as the formats allowable for their contributions to the museum (e.g., Do they have a choice of images, sound, student-produced videos/webcasts, etc.? What formats will you accept?).
- Provide students with clear instructions about time allotments, especially the amount of time for research versus production.
- Depending on the scope of the exhibit topics, allow anywhere from 1 day to 1 week each for research and production.
- Once complete, assemble all exhibits into a virtual museum and allow time for groups to celebrate, see, and offer feedback on each other's work.

Ideal for   Although the creation of a virtual museum lends itself to history and art (for example, a museum documenting political leadership over a period of time, a museum of natural history, or a museum dedicated to art of one form or another), a museum can be created for virtually any subject area. Other examples might include a museum of mathematical milestones, a museum of scientific advancements in chemistry, a museum of great English literature, etc.

Cautions   Although students should be encouraged to use research, it's important that they be mindful of copyright when contributing materials. This is especially critical if the museum is to be online, since the copyright holders could take issue with unauthorized use of their images and content. Students must cite their sources and link to rather than copy and paste materials.

5

Review Strategies

Chapter Introduction

This chapter provides you with a series of Review strategies—that is, the strategies encouraging students to actively summarize and clarify their learning, with emphasis on the key points. Keep in mind that research suggests *that at least 5%* of classroom time should be devoted to the review of learning.

Have your learning outcomes in mind as you view the Review strategies, and make note of those that will best support the subject area and the goals you have established for students. Some of these strategies are ideal for test or exam preparation at the end of a unit of study (in this way, they are summative reviews), whereas others are better suited for end-of-lesson reviews (as formative reviews).

As you make selections from this chapter to integrate into your teaching, try to vary the approaches to review over the course of the term or school year to allow students a variety of ways to express knowledge and interact with the curriculum. Teachers are encouraged to repeat the same Review strategies from time to time, with the goal that students will be able to master the forms of communication and application within the strategies through ongoing practice.

Refer to http://www.corwin.com/95strategies to see how each of these strategies aligns with the Common Core State Standards.

STRATEGY 68

Gallery Walk

Rationale   This strategy allows students to showcase their work, as well as to see how their peers approached similar work. Students learn from seeing examples and offering feedback and can reflect on improvement of their own work when feedback comes from peers.

Materials   Feedback Form (optional)

Description   At the end of a summative task, students display their projects or work in the classroom. The class is given a set time to walk around and view peers' work.

Consider incorporating feedback forms in front of each student's work, where peers can offer commendations or constructive suggestions as they visit one another's work.

Ideal for   Any summative task that includes a visual component (e.g., slides, poster, portfolio, booklet, brochure, etc.)

REPRODUCIBLE

Gallery Walk Feedback Form

Name of Reviewer: _____ Date: _____

Instructions

- Before starting, ensure that the names of peers or groups who displayed an item in the gallery are on your list.
- Review the criteria on which you'll be offering feedback.
- Each time you visit a station in the gallery, place a checkmark that you believe best reflects that work.
- Once you complete the gallery walk, return this sheet to your teacher.

Name or group reviewed	Criterion 1:				Criterion 2:				Criterion 3:			
	1	2	3	4	1	2	3	4	1	2	3	4

STRATEGY 69

Metaphorical Picnic

Rationale	Most students respond to creative tasks that allow them to actively participate in construction of understanding. This task allows students to share their learning with other groups by offering an expert summary in the form of a picnic dish.
Materials	Paper tablecloth hung on a display wall, paper plates, markers, tape or glue
Description	Introduce the topic by emphasizing that what makes a successful picnic is a variety of dishes brought by everyone participating. Explain that in this activity, students will create dishes to represent something they learned.
	Distribute paper plates to individuals or groups, and assign topics. Using markers, paper, and glue, students decorate the paper plate with words and/or images to summarize their assigned topic.
	Once complete, each plate is glued or taped to the paper tablecloth for display in the classroom.
Ideal for	End-of-unit or course review, where dishes can represent topics or units of study
Example	In a law class, each student creates a dish to summarize a key piece of legislation at course end. The dish should include the name of the legislation, the jurisdiction, points to illustrate the intent, and one case example.
Cautions	Students may need assistance in establishing criteria for the content of their dishes. Provide them with an example before they begin.

STRATEGY 70

Postcards

Rationale   Students learn more and are more engaged when they can construct understanding via active engagement and creation. This strategy helps students to build literacy while making sense of course content in the form of correspondence.

Materials   Cardboard cut to poster size, pens, glue, etc., or access to a computer lab if students create postcards electronically

Description   Individually or in groups, students create a postcard with a graphic image and a message to summarize an assigned topic/lesson/unit. It can be addressed to a real person or a fictional character from the course content.

Ideal for   End-of-unit review

STRATEGY 71

Cue Card Race

Rationale   This strategy offers an opportunity for students to engage in movement, which for some learners will engage and offer much-needed energy release. While competitive tasks are not for all learners, many respond favorably to the motivation that this type of review activity offers.

Materials   Provide index cards with answers; the teacher should have a list of questions. Ensure that there are more questions than students in the group so that everyone has an opportunity to participate.

Ample room for a race

Stations at which answer cards can be placed, one per team

Description Teacher creates a list of questions and puts down the answers on index cards, creating one set of answers per team. The index cards with answers are placed at stations around the room, with one station per team.

Each team of students is numbered so all are clear on the order in which they take turns.

Teacher reads out a question; the players for that round run to their team stations and select the correct answer from the cue cards.

The first student back with a correct answer receives a point for his or her team.

Ideal for   Any topic for which students should be able to derive a specific answer

Example   For a math lesson, set up stations for each team (for example, three tables at the far end of the room). Students line up within their teams, allowing for each student to have at least one turn at the race.

Teacher reads out a question, and the players for that round run to the stations and select the correct answer from the cue cards. The first one back with a correct answer receives a point.

Cautions   Ensure a safe and large space for students to participate.

Accommodate for learners who cannot participate in a race.

> **STRATEGY 72**
>
> *Peer Edit*

Rationale   Students learn from feedback and critique. Rather than submit work to the teacher directly, a peer edit allows students to offer feedback to one another. They learn from the strengths and improvements on others' work and also by revising their own work.

Materials   Peer Edit Checklist (optional)

Description   In pairs, triads, or quads, students edit one another's work.

Ideal for   Any topic that requires writing or visual representation

Cautions   Students should receive instruction on how to edit.

Teacher should collect peer edits and final products to ensure that students are indeed revising their work.

REPRODUCIBLE

Peer Edit Checklist

Reviewer Name: _____ Writer's Name: _____

Criteria	Yes	No	Comments
1. Is the work complete?			
2. Are there any spelling or grammatical errors?			
3. As a whole, is the purpose of the item clear?			
4. Is the presentation of information appropriate for the intended audience?			
5. Is the language clear?			
6. Does the content flow in an organized or logical manner?			
7. If this is a written composition, is there an introduction, a body, and a conclusion?			
8. If this is a written composition, does each paragraph start with a topic sentence, and is the body clearly tied to the topic sentence?			
9. Are the arguments made logical?			
10. Is there enough evidence or reasons to support claims the author makes?			

(Continued)

(Continued)

Other helpful comments or observations:

STRATEGY 73

Classroom Jeopardy

Rationale   Games can often be engaging ways to involve students in the curriculum. This variation of a popular television game show allows students to review material in the context of a large-group competition.

Materials   Electronic jeopardy game with a multimedia projector (many can be downloaded free of charge, or teachers can create one using presentation software) or paper jeopardy game fashioned from manila envelopes with the amounts on the outside and questions inside. The structure should be a series of categories with questions of five varying values for each category.

Buzzers (These can be electronic buzzers, bells, or flyswatters that can be tapped on a desk when a student is prepared to answer.)

Description   Have students play in three teams to involve everyone, and assign a scorekeeper and a host.

One representative from each team operates the buzzer for each round, rotating in whatever order the team prefers.

The correct response receives a score.

Ideal for   Any subject and especially for test preparation

Cautions   Not all students know the Jeopardy rules, so be sure to explain them and allow a practice round.

Be clear on whether you allow for team huddles before responding to questions or if the student at the buzzer must answer alone.

Be clear on whether you will deduct points for incorrect responses.

Have more questions than you need; sometimes this game goes quickly.

STRATEGY 74

Wheel of Fortune

Rationale   Games can often be engaging ways to involve students in the curriculum. This variation of a popular television game show allows students to review material in the context of a large-group competition.

Materials   Cardboard wheel with various point amounts, a bankrupt wedge, and some silly options

Set of review questions

Suction-cup ball that sticks to the wall when thrown

Description   Divide the class into teams, and assign a host and a scorekeeper.

Each team has a turn to throw the ball at the wheel and compete for that point level if a question is answered correctly.

Ideal for   End-of-unit reviews and test preparation

Cautions   Clearly explain the rules, and allow a practice round.

Have more questions than you think you need ready.

STRATEGY 75

Crossword

Rationale	Varying the ways in which students self-assess knowledge and prepare for tests and exams allows students to feel more confident in their understanding. While crossword puzzles do not suit everyone's preferences, some learners enjoy them immensely.
Materials	Create a crossword using an online puzzle maker or by hand.
Description	Students test their learning using a crossword puzzle.
	Consider allowing students to pair up and create crossword puzzles for one another.
Ideal for	Checking specific knowledge, including definitions
Cautions	Proofread your clues and answers carefully.

STRATEGY 76

Mind Map

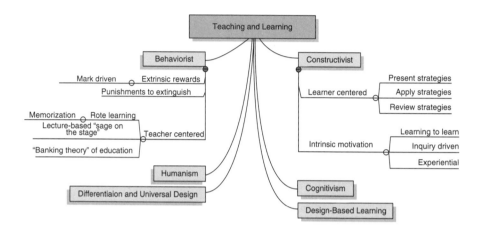

Rationale   Research reported in *Beyond Monet* suggests that mind mapping is an effective tool for learners to make connections across topics and themes and better retain their learning. This is particularly effective for the visual learner.

Materials   None

Description   Students create a visual organizer to connect various related concepts. This can be completed individually or in small groups, by hand or using specialized graphing software. A number of online tools are available to create mind maps.

Ideal for   The end of a chapter or unit

Cautions   Effective mind mapping takes practice. Model the process, and guide students throughout the term or school year.

STRATEGY 77

Word Web

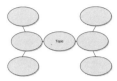

Rationale   Word webs are especially effective for visual learners, though they encourage all learners to explicitly make connections among vocabulary and concepts. This can be effective in retention when students recall those connections as they apply the vocabulary to new situations.

Materials   Paper, pens

Description   Similar to a mind map; students record connected words using a visual organizer. If a word wall is used, students can take the words from the wall and reorganize them to illustrate connections.

Ideal for   Virtually any topic

Cautions   Model the activity in advance for students.

REPRODUCIBLE

Word Web

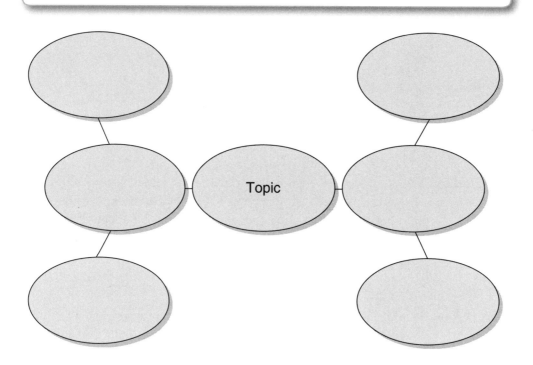

STRATEGY 78

List-Group-Label

Rationale   This is a strategy that calls on students to reflect on what they have learned and organize those components to make sense of it. This is particularly effective for kinesthetic and spatial learners since it requires working with physical materials and shuffling them around to make connections and understand the bigger picture.

Materials   Sticky notes, paper

Description   List: In groups, students record key terminology and concepts learned during the course of a chapter or unit of study.

Group: Next, groups arrange the sticky notes in order to create categories.

Label: On a sheet of paper, record the category name and arrange the sticky notes beneath it.

Students can then circulate and observe how their groupings compare with others and revise their work if necessary.

Ideal for   End-of-chapter or end-of-unit summation

STRATEGY 79

Thumbs Up/Thumbs Down

Rationale   This strategy provides teachers with a sense of students' learning at the end of a lesson; in addition, it gives an opportunity for students to learn from one another, provided the teacher asks for clarification.

Materials   Teacher-prepared statements (either true or false for determining learning or statements that require a level of agreement or disagreement) relating to the unit or topic studied

Description   Students respond with thumbs up for the affirmative, thumbs down for the negative, and thumbs horizontal for neutral or not sure in response to teacher statements.

Where some students responded incorrectly or were unsure, those who are confident in their learning should take a moment to explain the concept or issue to their peers.

Ideal for   Formative diagnostic assessment of students' understanding (when using true/false) or to introduce discussion (when using opinion-based statements)

STRATEGY 80

Wiki

Rationale Using technology—especially technology that students enjoy— can engage them and encourage them to build literacy skills in nontraditional ways. Using wikis for learning offers a productive way for students to enhance their collaboration skills, while contributing to the group's knowledge on a topic.

Materials Access to a computer lab

A wiki with access restricted to the class set up using an online wiki farm (a website that hosts wikis)

Description As a closing activity, students are responsible for recording all of their learning in a wiki for test or exam preparation. They should be required to edit one another's work. A portion of the wiki can be devoted to anticipating possible test or exam questions.

Ideal for Any topic

Cautions Students may require guidance on how to use a wiki.

To ensure participation, assign topics or sections to students and provide motivation for them to both post and edit.

STRATEGY 81

Storyboarding

Rationale   This strategy allows students to express their understanding, knowledge, and ideas in a nontraditional way and is especially engaging to individuals with artistic intelligence.

Materials   Storyboard templates, either as handouts on photocopied paper or on matte board

Description   Students create a storyboard to demonstrate their understanding of a historical event or a literary work. Each panel in the storyboard contains a visual representation of an important point or subevent and should be labeled with a brief description of what the visual represents.

Ideal for   The end of a historical study or a literary work with a plot

Cautions   Adapt the criteria to accommodate students' varied abilities to create drawings, or use this strategy as an option for differentiated instruction.

Storyboarding

Use the template below to create a storyboard. Create additional pages as you require them.

1.

2.

3.

4.

5.

6.

STRATEGY 82

What's the Big Idea?

Rationale   Students can easily lose a sense of focus at the end of a class or the school day. This simple strategy asks students to identify one big idea from the class or school day. This encourages reflection as well as critical thinking to distinguish important from less important information.

Materials   None

Description   Students identify and name a big idea from class. They should provide

- One to two points to justify their choice
- One to two points of supporting detail

This can be done on paper and handed in or verbally at the end of class. Students can be assigned to present the big ideas at the end of each class throughout the school year.

Ideal for   Any topic

STRATEGY 83

Cue Card Scramble

Rationale   Students benefit from applying abstract concepts to concrete examples. This strategy allows students to rotate through a number of sorting examples.

Materials   Index cards with examples and headings relevant to the topic, one set per small group or table group

Description   In groups, students arrange the cue cards in the appropriate order. Students rotate clockwise to each table to complete a variety of sorts.

Ideal for   Any topic for which a number of examples can be generated to help students demonstrate their knowledge

Example   For types of business ownership, headings would be *sole proprietor*, *partnership*, etc.; the examples would be McDonald's, Walmart, etc.

Cautions   Ensure that students scramble the cards once they have completed the sort in preparation for the next rotating group.

STRATEGY 84

Structured Sort

Rationale   Students benefit from applying abstract concepts to concrete examples. This strategy allows them to sort examples.

Materials   Concepts or parts of the topic on separate slips of paper that students sort and group together, one set per student or per group

Description   This is a form of graphic organizer, but all parts or concepts are on slips of paper, and students organize them. Students can work alone or in groups.

Ideal for   Topics that may have interrelated concepts (e.g., structure of a government), sequences (e.g., the plot of a book or play, the accounting cycle), etc.

Example   A cardboard timeline with important dates marked on it and cue cards representing historical events provide a good structured sort.

A set of cards representing the branches of the federal government would provide another structured sort.

STRATEGY 85

Graffiti Mural

Rationale   This strategy offers students an opportunity to express themselves in multiple ways and make sense of new material in a cooperative setting. Students have the opportunity to build on one another's work.

Materials   Large roll of craft paper or several sheets of chart paper, affixed to a classroom wall as a mural

Markers or crayons

Description   The entire class participates in creating a graffiti wall to represent collective learning. Provided the paper is long enough, the class can approach the mural and contribute their ideas about key learning or important concepts. Encourage students to build on one another's work.

Ideal for   End-of-unit review for any topic

Cautions   Some classes may require guidance to help them determine what sorts of graffiti contributions are meaningful. Teachers can begin by offering examples.

STRATEGY 86

Password

Rationale   Games can often be engaging ways to involve students in the curriculum. This variation of a popular television game show (*The Million-Dollar Pyramid*) allows students to review material in the context of a large-group competition.

Materials   Index cards with key terms from the lesson or unit of study

Timer

Description   Working in groups of three, students take turns giving clues, receiving clues, and observing. The object of the game is for the person receiving clues to guess the term as quickly as possible. The rules are as follows:

- The person receiving clues cannot see the term on the card.
- The person giving clues can only use one-word clues and no gestures.
- Each match cannot exceed 30 seconds and is timed by the buzzer or by the observer.

Ideal for   Any topic that has a multitude of terms

STRATEGY 87

Circle-Square-Triangle

Rationale   The geometric shapes provide students with an organizing formula to self-assess their reactions to a unit of study or lesson.

Materials   Handout with circle, square, and triangle shapes on which students can write their responses, or chart paper with large representations of the shapes on which groups can record their responses

Description   At the end of a lesson or a unit of study, students identify at least one of each:

- Circle: a question circling in your mind
- Square: something that squared with you (e.g., you understand it or it validated prior knowledge)
- Triangle: something you could use to form a basis for future learning

Students can debrief either in small groups or as a large class to identify themes and to answer their questions, or they can submit their responses to the teacher.

Ideal for   Any topic

Circle-Square-Triangle

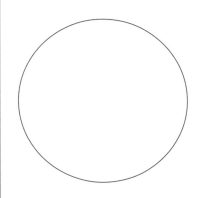

⇐ *Question(s) <u>circling</u> in your mind*

Something that <u>squared</u> with you ⇒

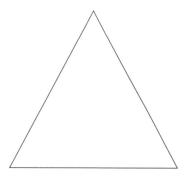

⇐ *Something that you can use as a basis for future application or learning*

STRATEGY 88

Broken Eggs

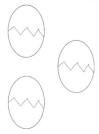

Rationale   This strategy allows students to move around while reviewing, as well as to work with peers to solve the problem of determining matches (and perhaps patterns, depending on the subject area).

Materials   For each term or concept, create an egg from paper with the term or concept on the top half and the definition or elaboration on the bottom half. Cut each egg in half, and shuffle.

Ensure that each student receives one half of the egg.

Description   Students match the two halves of broken eggs to assemble the concept or definition by finding the peer who holds the other half.

Ideal for   Knowledge/understanding tasks

Broken Eggs

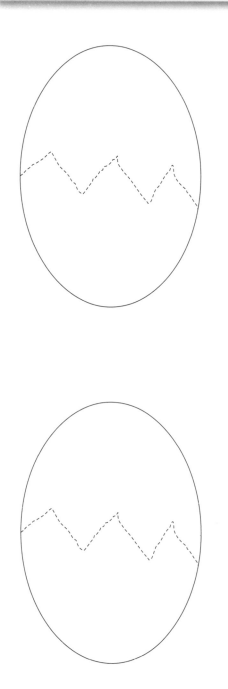

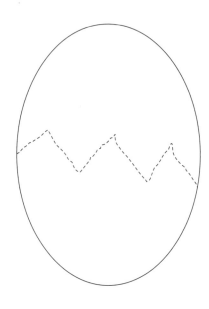

STRATEGY 89

Note Comparison

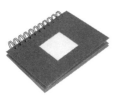

Rationale   By working together and reviewing one another's work, students practice deduction and analysis. This also helps them self-assess their own note taking and revise their work, which encourages continuous improvement.

Materials   None

Description   Students compare notes with a partner or in a small group and fill in any gaps or misunderstandings. To debrief, students share any unresolved questions or issues as a large group.

Ideal for   Courses or units in which students take notes

Cautions   In some cases, students should be grouped based on their note-taking ability so that those with more detailed notes can help those with less detailed notes.

Decide in advance the time span for students to compare notes (e.g., one class or the entire unit).

STRATEGY 90

Trade-a-Problem

Rationale   This strategy allows students to take full control of the review process by creating problems for their peers and practicing composing review questions. It also allows for cooperative learning and peer discussion to solve problems.

Materials   Index cards for students

Description   In small groups, students compose review questions on index cards, writing the answer on the back.

Groups trade cards and attempt to answer one another's questions by consensus without looking at the answer. If the group's answer does not agree with the original answer, they add their answer on the back of the card as an alternative.

Cards continue to be traded.

Finish the activity with a large group discussion focusing on questions with more than one answer.

Ideal for   Any unit or topic

STRATEGY 91

Mystery Interview

Rationale	Students learn from induction and questioning. This strategy allows students to engage in a questions process, which cultivates critical thinking and also allows students to use and/or develop their intrapersonal intelligences.
Materials	None
Description	Assign each student an identity. This identity could be a literary character, a mathematical formula, a historical figure, a country, etc.
	Pair students so that each interviews the other to determine his or her identity.
Ideal for	Almost any topic
Cautions	Give clear directions and demonstrate some sample questions (e.g., Am I a person? Am I a formula? Can I be used to solve an equation?) ahead of time.
	Provide lists of questions for younger or struggling students.

STRATEGY 92

Exit Cards and 3-2-1

Rationale   Students can benefit from having to reflect on a particular question or theme after learning has taken place as a reinforcer.

Materials   None

Description At the end of a class or the school day, each student completes an Exit Card with a particular question or prompt related to the day's learning before leaving.

A variation of the Exit Card is to have students respond with the 3-2-1 response:

- Three things they learned
- Two questions they still have
- One thing they enjoyed

Ideal for   Almost any topic

Examples   Any question can be used. Here are some generic examples not tied explicitly to the curriculum:

- List three things you learned in class today.
- What was the best part of today's class? Why?
- What was the most difficult thing you learned today?
- Evaluate your participation in class today. What did you do well? What will you do differently tomorrow?

STRATEGY 93

Living Image/Tableau

Rationale   Kinesthetic learners can make sense of learning, which allows for a performance using the body. By creating a living image or tableau, students have to consider the key people involved in a particular learning topic and how a visual representation can reflect a sequence of events.

Materials   None

Description   Ask students to reflect on either a historical event or a piece of literature they have completed studying. If photographs or drawings are available for an event, you may wish to share these with students.

Assign a subtopic or theme to groups of four or five students.

Students take 5 to 10 minutes to formulate their tableaux. Then, groups take turns presenting their tableaux to the class. After each tableau, the class can ask questions or ask for clarifications of the elements of the performance.

Ideal for   History, drama, or literature, though the strategy can be applied to other subjects as well

Examples   Create a tableau to represent a particular aspect of a job interview.

Create a tableau to represent an aspect of the Roaring Twenties (historical period).

STRATEGY 94

Human Sequence Line-Up

Rationale Kinesthetic learners can make sense of learning, which allows for a performance using the body. By using their bodies to represent abstract concepts, students will remember the placement of events or rules.

Materials None

Description Create cards with large print to represent event or components to be sequenced.

Provide each student with a card.

Allow the class time to organize themselves in the correct sequence. Encourage discussion and collaboration to get the sequence right.

Ideal for Any topic that has a sequence—whether a timeline or hierarchy of concepts to follow

Examples Historical timeline for World War II

The sequence of accounts in the ledger

Order of mathematical operations (for small groups)

STRATEGY 95

Definition Derby

Rationale   Through discussion, students can compare their understandings of definitions of key terms from a lesson or unit. Teachers can use this strategy as a means of seeing how their classes made sense of content.

Materials   Cards with key terms from the lesson or unit—one set per group

Description   In groups of three to five students, each student receives one or more cards facedown.

Students take turns sharing the definition without revealing the card, while their peers guess at which term is being defined. After each round of guessing, students should discuss if any elements are missing from the definition and what aspects of the definition given helped them make correct (or incorrect) guesses.

Ideal for   Any topic that has distinct terminology

Appendix A

Ideas for Grouping Students

Grouping students is an important consideration when applying cooperative learning strategies. This appendix provides you with a number of ideas for grouping students.

Keep in mind that at times, it is best to group students by ability—either homogeneous groupings for similar ability or based on complementary skills so that students can assist one another. Alternately, you can use quasi-randomized groupings in order to ensure that students work with different peers on different days. This appendix provides you with several approaches for both ability groupings and quasi-randomized groupings.

Numbering the Class

- Assign numbers by counting out the class (e.g., 1 through 5, then again at 1) and arrange the class by telling all 1's to meet in a certain place, all 2's to meet in another place, etc.

Find Your Other Half

- This is a grouping strategy based on the pedagogy of the same name (see Strategy 19 on page 55).
- For pairings, create cards with pairs of names or objects so that there are enough unique pairs for each student in the class. These might include peanut butter and jelly or Fred and Wilma Flintstone.
- Distribute the cards, and have students locate their other half.

Deck of Playing Cards

- In advance, determine if groups will be by numbers or suits. Remove unnecessary cards from a deck. Distribute cards to students, and instruct them to assemble.

Colored Paper

- Distribute pieces of colored paper to students, and have groups assemble by color.

Colored Clothespins

- If using the Clothesline strategy of instruction as an introduction (see Strategy 22 on page 58), consider distributing different-colored clothespins to students to establish groupings based on the color they receive.

Puzzle Pieces

- Using either a page from a magazine or a printed picture (one for each group), create jigsaw puzzle pieces, and allow the students to find the pieces that correspond to theirs to form the group.
- You may wish to put instructions for the activity on the reverse of the puzzle so that when members of the group find one another, they can assemble their puzzle in order to unlock the activity instructions.

Transportation Groupings

- Create a set of cards with different modes of transportation in graphic format (bicycle, train, automobile, airplane, horse, shoes), distributing one card to each student. Instruct students to locate the members of their group without using words.
- A variation on this is animal grouping, where cards depict a variety of animals (elephant, bird, lion, dog, cat, mouse, etc.). Distribute one card to each student. Instruct students to use only noises to locate their groups.

Random List Generation

- Use a random list generator (there are a number of these available online) to scramble the class list and create groups from the random sequence.

Strengths to Assign Group Roles

Once in a group, use students' strengths to assign their roles. For example:

- Best artist takes on Role 1.
- Best at getting things done takes on Role 2.
- Best at getting things done quickly takes on Role 3.
- Best at math takes on Role 4.
- First in class each day takes on Role 5.

Appendix B

Guide to Lesson Remodeling PLCs

C hapter 2 introduced the lesson remodeling process and offered a number of examples. Lesson remodeling can be performed individually, though collaborative remodeling through the formation of a professional learning community (PLC) offers teachers the opportunity to learn together and from each other while drawing on each other's perspectives. To facilitate collaborative remodeling, we offer a guide to how such PLCs can operate.

Because the specific way a given PLC operates will depend on the nature of the teachers who participate in the group, the school and district contexts of that PLC, and the amount of meeting time available, this guide supplies a range of possible approaches and options for structure, format, and content. PLCs should choose from the options offered here and modify them to suit their individual needs. In addition, members of the PLC might come up with unique approaches beyond those here to remodel lessons as a group. Without question, the options and approaches used by a particular PLC should be the ones that make the most sense to its members.

This guide also suggests ways in which PLC meeting leaders can model strategies for their peers, thus offering variety in the structure of the meeting, as well as examples of lived experience of the types of teaching/learning strategies that they might use in their classes.

Table B.1   Overview of PLC Suggestions

WHO	Teachers within the school or district who have common grade or level classes or common subject areas; the number of members can vary, but given that lesson remodeling is a dialogical process, teachers should work in triads or quads within the PLC. For each meeting, one PLC member should be designated as the leader.
WHAT	A PLC designed for peer learning through lesson remodeling
WHY	The purpose of the PLC is to remodel lessons in order to (a) meet Common Core State Standards and (b) contribute to student success through increased student engagement resulting from remodeled lessons.
WHEN	Members of the PLC should decide how often to meet based on time available to them and the needs of the group. At the very least, PLCs should meet formally twice per term, or six times per year, in order to apply lesson remodeling and have an opportunity to engage in professional reflection to discuss the results of the remodeled lessons in their classes. Keep in mind that formal meetings, as discussed below, can take a variety of formats. Using an online collaboration tool (such as a wiki or document-sharing site) can augment formal meetings and allow for informal communication and idea sharing among members throughout the school year.
WHERE	PLCs may take place in face-to-face settings, such as the school or district office. However, geographically diverse PLCs can take place using information and communication technologies. Online tools, including wikis and document-sharing sites, provide an excellent means for flexible participation.

Meeting 1: Laying the Groundwork

PLC member preparation

- PLC members will have read Chapters 1 and 2 of this book.

Materials

- Chart paper
- Markers
- Sticky notes
- Small sheets of paper or cutout clothing items (see reproducible for Strategy 22 on page 58)
- Clothespins
- String, twine, or ribbon affixed in the room for the "clothesline"
- Circle-Square-Triangle reproducible (see page 152)

Meeting objectives

By the close of this meeting, PLC members should have answers to the following questions:

- Where do I situate my pedagogical philosophy?
- How do the various approaches to pedagogy fit into my teaching style?
- How can the Present-Apply-Review (PAR) structure be best used in my subject area and grade level?

Total meeting time: 70 minutes

Agenda Item	Timing	Description
1. Welcome and Introductions	10 min	The PLC meeting leader welcomes the group, and members introduce themselves and state what they individually hope to achieve through PLC participation.
2. Collaborative Goal Setting	10 min	Using a modified Reflection Wall (see page 109 of this book), the PLC meeting leader distributes sticky notes, and each member records what he or she believes the PLC's goals ought to be. Members affix their sticky notes to a sheet of chart paper. As a group, members identify themes and arrive at three to five goals for the group.

(Continued)

(Continued)

Agenda Item	Timing	Description
3. Group Norms	15 min	The PLC meeting leader reminds the group that lesson remodeling requires both reflection and peer feedback. While this is an extremely valuable learning process, giving and receiving feedback can be delicate and sometimes uncomfortable. The PLC meeting leader then leads the group in establishing a set of guidelines for the PLC. These should include statements such as the following: • Maintain an environment of mutual respect, caring, integrity, and truthfulness. • Critique the lesson and not the individual when remodeling. • When offering feedback, balance positive and negative comments. • When receiving feedback, keep in mind that it is a process of professional learning, and feedback on lessons is not personal criticism.
4. Chapter 1 Review	15 min	Using the Whip-Around strategy (see Strategy 14 on page 50), the PLC meeting leader asks members to skim Chapter 1 and identify the words and phrases that garner a strong reaction from them. Then, the group rapidly reads their words and phrases. The PLC meeting leader asks what themes emerge, and members can discuss. Important highlights from Chapter 1 that might be mentioned include the following: • Constructivism requires that learning engage the student in meaning making through active participation in the process. • The PAR format points to optimal use of classroom time established through research. The greatest proportion of time should be spent on students' application of concepts and skills.
5. Chapter 2 Review	15 min	The PLC meeting leader distributes copies of the Circle-Square-Triangle reproducible and allows members several moments to jot down their notes. In pairs (see Strategy 36, Think-Pair-Share, on page 84), members can share their responses. Allow time for the group to raise any questions left unanswered and discuss solutions. Important highlights from Chapter 2 that might be mentioned include these: • Remodeling can help us make the transition from *habitual practice* to *intelligent practice*, or moving from active knowing to cognitive knowing.

Agenda Item	Timing	Description
		• This approach to remodeling incorporates design-down planning, such that we begin with the student learning outcomes, expectations, and standards; design the assessment; and then create a PAR structured lesson. We can tweak existing lessons through remodeling by putting them into the framework.
6. Next Steps	5 min	Establish the date, time, and location for the next meeting if it has not been determined.

The PLC meeting leader explains that remodeling will begin in the next session using the core concepts just reviewed, so members should bring their copy of this book, as well as a lesson they would like to collaboratively remodel with their peers. The group may opt for triads or quads to exchange lessons in advance to allow for prereading. |

Follow-up

- At the end of the meeting, the PLC meeting leaders should keep copies of the goals and norms established to display at future meetings. Norms can be affixed to chart paper for safekeeping.
- If PLC members decide to exchange lessons prior to the next meeting, they should do so at a mutually agreeable date before the next meeting.

Meeting 2 (and All Subsequent Even-Numbered Meetings): Remodeling

PLC member preparation

- PLC members will bring copies of a lesson they wish to remodel to the group, with enough copies for their triad or quad. It's a good idea to exchange lessons in advance of the meeting to allow members to read and reflect on them, though this might not be feasible.
- PLC members will bring their copies of this book for reference during the meeting.

Materials

- Chart paper listing the goals and group norms established in the first meeting, posted prominently
- Copies of the reproducible lesson plan template (see page 175) for PLC members to take notes
- Pens
- Sticky notes

Meeting objectives

By the close of this meeting, PLC members should have answers to the following questions:

- How can I remodel lessons?
- How can strategies be adapted and improved using this book?

Total meeting time: 110 minutes, which can be completed as one session or over two consecutive sessions

Agenda Item	Timing	Description
1. Getting Started	10 min	The PLC meeting leader reminds the group of the goals and the group norms established in the first meeting. Next, the PLC meeting leader should reveal this meeting's objectives and the agenda. Members will participate in the same triads or quads as at the previous meeting.

Agenda Item	Timing	Description
2. Lesson Remodel: Practice Round	10 min	As a large group, members rapidly practice a lesson remodel using any one of the examples in this book (see the Examples section beginning on page 18). To do this, the PLC meeting leader directs them to the lesson most appropriate for this group, and a volunteer reads the original lesson aloud. The PLC meeting leader indicates that this is the descriptive round in the process.
3. Lesson Remodel: Descriptive Round	10 min	Working in triads or quads, members exchange lessons and read over their peers' work without commenting or judging. This task is purely descriptive. At the end of 10 minutes of reading time, triads or quads may ask questions about one another's work for clarification (without probing).
4. Lesson Remodel: Interpretive Round	10 min	Once triads or quads have read at least one partner's lesson in the group, they begin an interpretive round. In this round, the small groups discuss the existing lessons: • Why did members select these lessons? • What are the perceived and/or observed strengths and weaknesses? • Are there any class-contextual factors that need to be considered in the remodeling process? The amount of time needed to examine the work depends on the lesson complexity and number of PLC members in small groups.
5. Lesson Remodel: Revision Round	30 min	The PLC meeting leader distributes templates, pens, and sticky notes to groups, which they can use to remodel. Working with at least one triad or quad member's lesson, the peer remodels it by 1. Reviewing the assessment task for design-down planning evidence and for student engagement 2. Organizing the lesson into the PAR framework and ensuring optimal timing for each component 3. Analyzing each existing strategy and considering what revisions or alternatives could be offered to increase the level of student centeredness, engagement, and attention to diverse learner needs. Members should be looking to the strategies in this book for PAR ideas.

(Continued)

(Continued)

Agenda Item	Timing	Description
6. Lesson Remodel: Reflective Round	30 min	Once the revisions have been completed, triads or quads then present their peers with the remodeled lessons, taking turns explaining what revisions they suggest and why. This should be an open discussion in which all members contribute to making meaning, ask questions, and offer suggestions in a respectful manner.
7. Next Steps	10 min	The PLC meeting leader thanks all members for their participation and explains that members ought to try out some ideas from today's session before the next meeting.

Follow-up

- Teachers should test out the remodeled lessons in their classes and note observations to bring to the next meeting.

Meeting 3 (and All Subsequent Odd-Numbered Meetings): Reflection and Revision

PLC member preparation

- PLC members will bring their copies of this book for reference during the meeting.

Materials

- Chart paper of the goals and group norms established in the first meeting, posted prominently
- Copies of the reproducible Did Well/Do Better (see page 176) organizer

Meeting objectives

By the close of this meeting, PLC members should have answers to the following questions:

- Which remodeling strategies were effective? Which were not? Why?
- Based on my experience since the last meeting, how can I remodel lessons more effectively?

Total meeting time: 60 minutes

Agenda Item	Timing	Description
1. Getting Started	10 min	The PLC meeting leader reminds the group of the goals and the group norms established in the first meeting. Next, the PLC meeting leader should reveal this meeting's objectives and the agenda. It's important that members be aware of the steps in the collaborative process in advance, so these should be made clear.
		If the PLC is large, members should self-select into triads or quads for small group work.
		The PLC meeting leader may be involved in a triad or quad but is responsible for maintaining the timing.

(Continued)

(Continued)

Agenda Item	Timing	Description
2. Did Well/ Do Better	15 min	The PLC meeting leader distributes copies of Did Well/ Do Better (see page 176) and asks members to jot down their thoughts based on their experience with the remodeling process, as well as using remodeled lessons in their practice. Using Think-Pair-Square, small groups discuss their responses. The PLC meeting leader facilitates a large-group debrief on any important insights or questions remaining.
3. Triad/Quad Debrief	20 min	Returning to their triads or quads, members engage in a detailed debrief and reflection about the process of remodeling and share specific examples of what occurred when they used their remodeled lessons in class. Where possible, they should think about how the revisions impacted student engagement and student achievement.
4. Group Debrief	15 min	Once groups have had sufficient time to discuss and reflect, the PLC meeting leader facilitates a large-group session with the intent of planning for the next meeting based on lessons learned from this round of remodeling. Finally, the PLC meeting leader establishes the dates and expectations for the next meeting given the suggestions for changes just arrived at.

Follow-up

- The next meeting will resume remodeling. Prior to that meeting, teachers should select the next lesson that they will bring for remodeling. If members have decided to exchange lessons in advance, they should do so by a mutually agreeable date.

Reproducible: Lesson Plan Template

Teacher:	
Subject/Grade	
Expectations/Outcomes	
Common Core State Standards	

Original Lesson	**Remodeled Lesson**
Assessment or Performance Task	Assessment or Performance Task
Present Strategies	Present Strategies
Apply Strategies	Apply Strategies
Review Strategies	Review Strategies

Reproducible: Did Well/Do Better

Did Well	Do Better

References

Bennett, B., & Rolheiser, C. (2008). *Beyond Monet: The artful science of instructional integration.* Toronto, Canada: Bookation.

Blakemore, S., & Choudhury, S. (2006). Development of the adolescent brain: Implications for executive function and social cognition. *Journal of Child Psychology and Psychiatry, 47*(3), 296–312.

Dale, E. (1969). *Audiovisual methods in teaching* (3rd ed.). New York, NY: Dryden Press.

Gardiner, L. F. (1998, Spring). Why we must change: The research evidence. *Thought & Action: The NEA Higher Education Journal,* 121–138.

Hyde, P. S., Falls, K., Morris, J. A., & Schoenwald, S. K. (2003). *Turning knowledge into practice: A manual for behavioral health administrators and practitioners about understanding and implementing evidence-based practices.* Boston, MA: The Technical Assistance Collaborative, Inc.

McTighe, J., & Thomas, R. S., (2003). Backward design for forward action. *Educational Leadership, 60*(5), 52–55.

Michaelsen, L. K., Fink, L. D., & Knight, A. (1997). Designing effective group activities: Lessons for classroom teaching and faculty development. In D. DeZure (Ed.), *To Improve the Academy,* (Vol. 16, pp. 373–397). Stillwater, OK: New Forums Press.

Moersch, C. (1998). Enhancing students' thinking skills: Exploring model technology-integration sites. *Learning and Leading With Technology, 25*(6), 50–53.

National Governors Association Center for Best Practices and the Council of Chief State School Officers. (2010). *Common core state standards for English language arts and literacy in history/social studies, science, and technical subjects.* Washington, DC: Author.

O'Neil, J. (1995). On schools as learning organizations: A conversation with Peter Senge. *Educational Leadership, 52*(7), 20–23.

Petty, G. (2009). *Evidence based teaching: A practical approach* (2nd ed.). London, England: Nelson Thornes.

Rushton, S., & Rushton, A. J. (2008). Classroom learning environment, brain research, and the No Child Left Behind initiative: Six years later. *Early Childhood Education, 36,* 87–92.

Smyth, J. (1994). The practical and political dimensions of teaching. *Education Links, 43,* 4–8.

Stiggins, R. (2005). From formative assessment to assessment for learning: A path to success in standards-based schools. *Phi Delta Kappan, 87*(4), 324–328.

Tate, M. L. (2010). *Worksheets don't grow dendrites.* Thousand Oaks, CA: Corwin.

van Duijvenvoorde, A. C. K., Zanolie, K., Rombouts, S. A. R. B., Raijmakers, M. E. J., & Crone, E. A. (2008). Evaluating the negative or valuing the positive? Neural mechanisms supporting feedback-based learning across development. *Journal of Neuroscience, 28*(38), 9495–9503. doi: 10.1523/JNEUROSCI.1485-08.2008

van Manen, M. (1995). On the epistemology of reflective practice. *Teachers and Teaching: Theory and Practice, 1*(1), 33–50.

Vescio, V., Ross, D., & Adams, A. (2008). A review of research on the impact of professional learning communities on teaching practice and student learning. *Teaching and Teacher Education, 24,* 80–91.

Vygotsky, L. S. (1978). *Mind and society: The development of higher psychological processes.* Cambridge, MA: Harvard University Press.

Wood, F. H., & Killian, J. E. (1998). Job-embedded learning makes the difference in school improvement. *Journal of Staff Development, 19*(1), 24–26.

Index

CORWIN
A SAGE Company

The Corwin logo—a raven striding across an open book—represents the union of courage and learning. Corwin is committed to improving education for all learners by publishing books and other professional development resources for those serving the field of PreK–12 education. By providing practical, hands-on materials, Corwin continues to carry out the promise of its motto: **"Helping Educators Do Their Work Better."**